Parris Island Planner

A GUIDE TO KEEPING YOUR SANITY WHILE YOUR LOVED ONE IS COMPLETING MARINE CORPS BOOT CAMP

Vera Basilone

https://parrisisland.com

Basil1, LLC

Parris Island Planner: A guide to keeping your sanity while your loved one is completing Marine Corps boot camp By Vera Basilone

Published by Basil1, LLC, P.O. Box 5259, Parris Island, SC 29905

Limit of Liability/Disclaimer of Warranty

Ebook: ISBN-13: 978-0-9996251-0-1

Paperback: ISBN-13: 978-0-9996251-1-8

Edited by Katie Chambers

Cover designed by Ida Fia Sveningsson

About the Author

For over eight years Vera Basilone has maintained the website ParrisIsland.com where she writes, edits and answers questions about Parris Island. As a Marine's wife, she accompanied her husband, GySgt Basilone, to his various duty stations throughout his career: 2nd Marine Division, Camp Lejeune, NC; 1st Marine Division, Camp Pendleton, CA; both Marine Corps Recruit Depots; FMF PAC, Pearl Harbor; and MCLB Albany, GA. At each location, she observed the unique challenges and opportunities faced by the Marines.

After her husband retired from the Marine Corps, she worked at the Marine Corps Recruit Depot for over nine years as an information technology contract worker. Vera received her bachelor's degrees from the University of South Carolina Aiken and Georgia Southwestern University. She lives in Beaufort, South Carolina, with her husband, Michael and Mr. Winston, the dachshund.

Author's Acknowledgments

My deepest gratitude to my husband, Michael, who has been patient and supportive, helping me with edits, corrections and information concerning the Marine Corps. It is rare to have a husband who is not only intimately connected to the writer's subject matter but competent in word structure and grammar. This book would not have been possible without his help.

My daughter, Nicole, who listened to me as I endlessly talked about people who visited my site and my dreams for other books and projects. Her creative mind and thoughtful advice always helped me move in the right direction.

Our dachshund, Mr. Winston, who was my constant companion throughout the day as I wrote, re-wrote and read my manuscript to him again and again. Through it all, he remained easy going and loving.

My editor, Katie Chambers, for turning my book into a polished work worthy of publication! Writers need professional editors and I am so glad I found one.

Ida Fia Sveningsson, owner of IF Design, who designed a fabulous looking book cover.

Jaime Masters, the Eventual Millionaire, who encouraged me to create an eBook and answered endless questions regarding how to move forward with my business. I would also like to acknowledge all of the Millionaire Hustlers who continue to provide support and answers to my business questions.

The Marines who helped me gain experience and information: Brigadier General Austin "Sparky" Renforth Commanding General, Marine Corps Recruit Depot Parris Island and Eastern Recruiting

Region; Lieutenant Colonel Stephen D. Bates, Executive Officer; SSgt Jose Nava, Marketing and Public Affairs Chief; Cpl Adeline Smith and LCpl Jack Rigsby, combat photographers from the 6th Marine Corps Recruiting District, Parris Island; Captain Alan W. Keith, Assistant Operations Officer; Drill Instructors SSgt Simone King and SSgt Lewis from the Recruit Training Regiment, Parris Island; and Sgt. Tony Simmons, Marketing and Public Affairs Representative, Recruiting Station Jacksonville, FL. I cannot thank them enough for the experiences and information I gained while participating in the wonderful 2017 Educator's Workshop. I would also like to thank Captain Flores, Director, Office of Communication, Parris Island, who took time to answer questions about 4th Phase.

Natalie Sisson, the Suitcase Entrepreneur, who offered tips on writing, video chats with successful writers and three months of Pomodoro sessions when I took part in her experiment, Write the Damn Book. Ali Luke, author of Publishing E-Books for Dummies, offered her fabulous critiquing talents, writing challenges and weekly chats as part of Writer's Huddle. My book coach, Scott Allan, for giving me insight and tips on the best way to accomplish my goals. And to Chandler Bolt and everyone at Self-Publishing School who helped me take the book from a written manuscript to a published work available online.

Last, but not least, all of the online entrepreneurs whose blog posts and informational podcasts motivated me to keep pushing forward even on those days when I wanted to abandon the site and read a lovely book! People like Pat Flynn, Leslie Samuel and Scott Barlow whose inspiration and advice worked.

Contents

Dedicated to the few, the proud and their families.

With the new day comes new strength and new thoughts

Eleanor Roosevelt

Introduction

My writing is simple and straightforward. I hope you will find my book an enjoyable read and a useful planner as you wait for the transformation of your recruit into a United States Marine. As a general convention, in place of "he/she" pronouns I use "he" throughout the book when referring to recruits. If you are reading the paperback version of this book all reference links can be found on parrisisland.com/links.

Who Should use this Planner?

When a loved one joins the Marine Corps, you have many questions swimming in your head and a lot of different emotions. Not knowing what to expect, you may turn to the internet but then feel overwhelmed by the amount of information and your lack of understanding. This information, which may or may not be correct, coupled with mystifying terms may leave you with even more questions.

If you can relate, and your loved one is going to boot camp on Parris Island or has already begun the journey, then this planner is for you. It contains everything I know about the process of Marine Corps Recruit Training and the answers to all of the questions people have asked me over the years.

Rather than focus on the recruit, as much of the information found online and in books does, **this planner engages the loved ones who wait for their recruits to complete training**. It also provides specific activities in the form of **Adapt and Overcome Action Steps** at the end of each chapter designed to prepare you for your visit to Parris Island.

After you finish reading, you will feel confident and informed as you make plans to visit Parris Island for your loved one's graduation.

This book contains three sections:

- How to prepare for your new role as a support person for your recruit.

- All the facts and answers to your questions about Marine Corps boot camp and the process of making Marines.

- How to prepare to attend a recruit graduation—all the valuable information you need to make the most of your trip.

My credentials

As the wife of a Marine for over 37 years, I've experienced being on the sideline from the time my husband entered boot camp until his retirement from the Marine Corps. I've sent letters and care packages and figured out the best way to spend my time as I waited for my husband to return home from various assignments and unaccompanied deployments. As the President of Basil1, LLC, I've written and answered questions about Parris Island for the last eight years on the website ParrisIsland.com.

Before writing this planner, I spoke with readers of ParrisIsland.com and asked them what challenges they had faced and what would have made the process easier for them. Using their responses as a guide, I compiled all the information you need in one easy to understand planner.

Navigating this book

This book is designed so you can jump to the information relevant to you. If your loved one is already in Phase 2 of training, look at the table of contents and skip to chapters in section two. If your recruit's graduation day is approaching, look at section three to help organize your trip.

Section 1: Your Loved One is going to Boot Camp, Now What?

In this section, you will learn the basics about the USMC Recruiters. Who are they? When should you reach out to the Recruiter and what kind of questions should you ask? You will see what is included in the recruiting process but from a loved one's perspective. This part shows you how to write letters, what to send and what not to send. It also includes a chapter on military time and a chapter on recruit battalions.

Section 2: Boot Camp: Everything You Wanted to Know but Didn't Know How to Ask

Section two gives you a detailed look at recruit training and what your loved one is going through during each step. You will understand the Training Matrix and details about the training your recruit receives week by week. Each chapter includes action items so you can take an involved role in increasing your recruit's moral.

Section 3: Getting Ready for Graduation Day

Section three is all about visiting Parris Island. It contains the answers to many of your questions: What do I do before I leave home? What should I expect when I arrive at Parris Island? What should I bring? Am I prohibited from taking specific items on base?

The rest of the section acquaints the reader with things to see and do while visiting Parris Island and what goes on during graduation day events. Sprinkled throughout the book, you will find links to valuable resources.

The contents of this book will save you time and make your life less stressful as you wait for your recruit to finish training. Each chapter will give you new insight into the boot camp process from a loved one's point of view. The Adapt and Overcome Action Steps will help you stay connected to your recruit and prepare you for your trip to Parris Island.

Your Free Bonus Gift!

As a thank you for purchasing the Parris Island Planner I am giving you a bonus gift:

The workbook includes checklists and worksheets to go along with the Adapt and Overcome Action Steps in the planner. To get your workbook go to the web address below.

https://www.parrisisland.com/workbook/

SECTION 1

Your Loved One is going to Boot Camp, Now What?

Blvd de France (photo by Vera Basilone)

Notes

CHAPTER 1

USMC Primer

Marine recruits cite pride, honor, self-discipline and being part of an elite unit are the primary reasons they join.

2017 Educator's Workshop Command Brief

Chapter Questions:

- What is the role of the USMC recruiter in the lives of a recruit?
- How do you talk to the recruiter?
- Are there things the recruiter doesn't want you to know?
- Under what circumstances can recruits receive a higher salary during boot camp?

The USMC Recruiter

The recruiter must find qualified candidates and screen out disqualified candidates. To do this, he evaluates the whole person. Does the applicant fall within the Marine Corps primary target market: young men and women ages 17 to 21? Are they in the top ten percent of all high school graduates? How did they do on their ASVAB (Armed Services Vocational Aptitude Battery)?

Recruiters look at ASVAB scores in three main categories:

1. Mental - Ninety-nine percent of applicants graduated high school. Over 70% received the highest score in the top three categories (mental, moral and physical) on the ASVAB.

2. Moral - The recruiter will disqualify applicants with severe drug use, problems with the police, or undesirable tattoos.

3. Physical - All applicants must pass a medical exam and the IST (initial strength test), consisting of a 1.5-mile run, pull-ups or push-ups and plank or crunches.

Overall, only 29% of the targeted individuals meet USMC standards and can enlist.

How to Talk to the Marine Corps Recruiter

If your loved one has not signed up for the Marine Corps yet or is still in the poolee phase (a poolee is someone who is part of the delayed entry program waiting to go to boot camp), it is not too late to start a rapport with his recruiter. The recruiter can answer many of the questions you have about your loved one's enlistment: What type of MOSs (Military Occupational Specialties) are available in the Marine Corps? What do you do if someone becomes ill or passes away and you need to get a message to your recruit during basic training?

How Should You Contact The Recruiter?

Your recruit should have a phone number and e-mail address for his recruiter. If not, you can always look up the nearest recruiting station online for general information. Since recruiters are out of the office meeting prospective recruits, you should email them your general questions. They carry digital devices such as smart phones and laptops and you will most likely receive a quicker answer via email. Make sure you give the recruiter a few days to respond. If you don't receive a reply, send a second e-mail request or follow-up with a phone call and voice message.

Three Things Your Recruiter Doesn't Want You to Know

As mentioned above, the recruiter's job is to find qualified candidates for the Marine Corps. Once identified, the recruiter will explain the positive aspects of boot camp training.

He may leave out a few minor details about boot camp:

1. During the first phase of boot camp, your loved one may become distraught. When a first-time recruit steps onto the yellow footprints, he will think, "What on Earth did I get myself into?" Those thoughts linger during the first phase of boot camp as the individual is challenged both physically and mentally. Fortunately, you can play an active role in keeping the blues away by writing letters of encouragement (See chapter 2). Also, talk to your loved one about enlisting with a buddy. Many Marines I've spoken with admit having a friend, whom they already knew, enlist at the same time to provide comfort and encouragement.

2. Your loved one may become sick or injured in boot camp. The physical challenges are rigorous, and although drill instructors continually check for safety, accidents happen. A recruit may fall off an obstacle course challenge and land the wrong way on an ankle or arm.

All Female recruits go to Parris Island; males located east of the Mississippi are sent to Parris Island while the rest go to the Marine Corps Recruit Depot in San Diego. Here they live in close quarters for 13 weeks. Colds and "recruit crud" are common occurrences. It is important that your recruit notifies their drill instructors if he has a temperature or thinks he has more than a common cold. Many times recruits don't want the DI's to know they are sick. If a recruit misses too many training days, he may be recycled, put back into basic training with another platoon. Being recycled, while discouraging, is much better than becoming seriously ill. Make sure your loved one understands this and reports any health concerns.

3. Boot camp isn't the hardest part of being a Marine—support doesn't end after graduation. Speak with any Marine and they will tell you boot camp is the easy part. After your loved one is a Basically Trained Marine, he will move on to more training and then new duty stations with new challenges. Some of those duty stations will be far away from loved ones.

During boot camp, drill instructors manage every hour of every day. After boot camp, new Marines are expected to manage their own time. They are expected to schedule additional training to pick up rank, set up moves to new duty stations and keep a healthy work and family life balance.

While they can manage these challenges, their physical distance from friends and family for extended periods of time can take a toll on their psyche. Even when they have support from family, they need reaffirmation that they are loved. Way back in the 1980's, the Marine Corps stationed my husband in Okinawa, Japan. He would call me every two weeks, and we would talk for about an hour. We didn't have the internet, and phone calls from Japan cost $1.00 per minute. Between calls, Mike's parents and I would send him care packages and letters. Time crawled along, and all appeared to be well. About eight months through Mike's tour, he called at his usual time. After our typical small talk, he told me about the Marines whose marriages ended. Four of his buddies were now divorced. He paused for a short time and then asked, "Everything is okay with us, right?" These thoughts occupy the minds of our loved ones late at night.

Adapt And Overcome Action Steps:
- ☐ Find out who recruited your loved one.
- ☐ Think of five questions to ask.

☐ Call your recruiter and schedule a time to meet and ask questions.

Can a Marine Recruit Receive E-2 Pay While Going through Boot Camp?

What Does E-2 Mean?

E-2 is the pay grade for a Private First Class (PFC). It is one pay grade higher than E-1, the pay grade for a Private. Higher rank equals additional pay. Always check to see if your recruit qualifies for PFC pay during boot camp.

Under What Conditions May A Recruit Receive E-2 Pay In Boot Camp?

According to local recruiting personnel, Marine Recruits may receive E-2 pay throughout training if they meet any one of the following requirements:

- Possess an associate's degree from an accredited College/University
- Earned 15 semester hours or 22 quarter hours of college classroom work
- Participated in high school JROTC (Junior Reserve Officers' Training Corps) for at least two years
- Obtained E-5 rank in the Young Marines
- Received his Eagle Scout (or she received her Gold Award as a Girl Scout)
- Provided two referrals who join the Marine Corps

Opportunities change from time to time so check with your local recruiter on ways your loved one can receive E-2 pay while in boot camp. Along with additional income, the recruit will receive a promotion and graduate as a PFC (Private First Class). The promotion gives them additional time in grade (TIG), which will help them get promoted to Lance Corporal (E-3 pay grade) faster.

Adapt And Overcome Action Steps:

- ☐ During your appointment with the recruiter, ask him about E-2 pay for your loved one.

Summary of Main Points:

- Talk with your loved one's recruiter and ask the right type of questions.
- Discuss the way your loved one may struggle during boot camp.
- See if your loved one qualifies for E-2 pay.

Once you have completed the action steps, you will want to learn boot camp basics and help your recruit deal with the process while he is at Parris Island.

CHAPTER 2

The Basics

A good leader inspires people to have confidence in the leader; a great leader inspires people to have confidence in themselves...

Eleanor Roosevelt

Chapter Questions:
- How do I write to my recruit?
- What can I send to my recruit?
- How can I understand military time?
- What are the battalion colors?

Your Loved One made it to Parris Island, Now What?

Waiting for the Call

Your loved one is on his way to boot camp. When he arrives on Parris Island, he will make one call to let someone know he reached the recruit depot safely. Since the recruits line up next to 16 phones all a foot away from each other, your recruit will shout the scripted message:

"This is Recruit [Insert Last Name]. I have arrived safely at Parris Island. Please do not send me any food or bulky items in the mail. I will contact you in seven to nine days by letter with my new address. Thank you for your support. Goodbye for now."

Your recruit will not be able to say anything else, and he will end the call as soon as he finishes reading the script located inside the phone case. Nothing prohibits you from saying a quick, "love you" as your recruit rattles off the speech, but do not be upset when your loved one cannot acknowledge anything you say. And realize you may not have an opportunity to say anything before he hangs up. Keep a notepad close by and jot down things you wanted to say so you can include them in your next letter.

Writing Letters

Recruits are not permitted to have cell phones, computers or any type of internet access while in boot camp. Your loved one will not receive any news from the outside world: no Facebook, no email, no television and no social media of any type. This is why you should write him lots of letters while you wait for graduation day.

As mentioned above, it will take seven to nine days for you to receive a letter from your recruit with his address. A week or more may seem like a long time when you are waiting for word, but you can keep busy by writing letters beforehand. As soon as your loved one leaves for boot camp, you can begin composing your first letter. Make sure you date these letters and get them ready to send. Once you have the address, you can group several days in the same envelope or put them in separate envelopes. Just remember not to go over the acceptable amount of postage for a one-ounce letter. Drill instructor's hone in on anything unusual, like large decorated packages. Once a DI sees an oversized envelope, your recruit may receive incentive training (also called IT). Incentive training is usually extra physical activity. To keep your recruit off the drill instructor's radar, do not send more than two oz. of mail in one envelope at a time.

What Should You Write About?

You can write about all kinds of things, starting with normal activities like walking the dogs or something funny the cat did. Then add things that are happening in your hometown.

When a new Marine arrives home after boot camp, he may feel disconnected since he missed many things during his time away: friends married, sports teams won and lost games, people moved away, businesses closed, new business sprung up, etc. To keep your recruit connected, include information about the world around you:

- Local high school basketball, baseball or other sports. Find out how the teams are doing and write a paragraph or two about them. My husband, Mike, especially loved getting his high school's football scores from his dad.
- Local news
- Hometown tidbits—add articles from the newspaper about fairs or funny happenings around the town.
- Friends and family—send tasteful pictures.
- His former place of employment. Did he work at a local store or diner before going into the corps? If so, find out who continues to work there. Did anyone leave for a better job? Is the business doing well? Maybe they have new competitors down the street.
- His favorite TV show—tell him what is going on with the characters that week.
- New movies—give brief plot summaries.
- Information from his friends on Facebook—if you can see his wall, transcribe or take screenshots, then print and send them along in your next letter. Be careful not to send anything too controversial.

Keep your letters positive and supportive. Recruits go through quite a bit of stress during training. You can minimize anxiety by giving words of encouragement throughout the process:

- Let him know you miss him but you honor and support his decision to join the Marine Corps.
- Add inspirational quotes to your letters.
- Write down the words of his favorite uplifting songs. He can read the lyrics and play the song in his head. It will help him stay optimistic.

Ask questions about events found on the Training Matrix (https://www.mcrdpi.marines.mil/Recruit-Training/Recruit-Training-Matrix/). Learning to decipher the matrix is covered in chapter 3. Ask him about the other recruits in his platoon. Then ask him to describe a typical day. Do your best to keep letters upbeat, but if something terrible happens that can't wait, contact your local Red Cross, and they will get the message to your recruit.

What to Send

Always remember, anything you send that brings attention to your recruit is bad and may cause additional incentive training. For example, as a basic rule, do not send food unless your recruit asks for something specific, especially don't send protein bars. According to Capt. Alan W. Keith, RTR Assistant Operations Officer, Drill Instructors issue their recruits one protein bar a day. Males get Cliff bars; females receive Luna bars. Since your recruit attends dietary classes teaching him how to eat correctly and he enjoys food at the chow hall, designed to give recruits a well-balanced meal, he does not need any food you would send. I've eaten at the chow hall, and the food is delicious, especially after hours of exercise and classes.

Adapt and Overcome Action Steps:
- ☐ If your recruit has not left for boot camp, ask about his favorite songs. If he is at boot camp already, choose an

upbeat song that has meaning for you. You can search for song names and lyrics online. Transcribe the words or print them out. Include a note at the bottom telling him why you chose the song and what it means to you.

☐ Make sure you have a pen, postage, stationary and plain white envelopes.

☐ Write your first letter today.

☐ Talk about what happens around town. Remember to offer encouragement and keep your letters upbeat.

How to Tell Military Time

Soon after your loved one decided to join the Marine Corps, you will start hearing military time. Maybe you asked, "What time will you be home from the game?" only to be perplexed by the reply, "Around 1900." I remember some of the Marines giving me tutorials. "It is easy," they would say, "Just count back 2 and take off the 1." Their advice never made sense to me. However, you can learn how to tell military time with a few simple tips.

The 24-hour clock has been around for a long time, but according to Wikipedia, the U.S. Navy began using it in the 1920s. The clock runs from midnight to midnight starting at 0000 hours and ending at 2359 hours.

If you see 0100—which is pronounced "oh one hundred" or "zero one hundred hours"—the time is 1:00 a.m.; 0200 is 2:00 a.m. and so on up until noon which is 1200 hours. For example, if someone says, "The recruit graduation starts at 0900," you would know that means 9:00 a.m. If they say 0735, that would be 7:35 a.m. However, once you get past 1259, the next number is 1300 which is pronounced "thirteen hundred," and means 1:00 p.m. 1400 is 2:00 p.m. and so on.

Don't say, "Meet me at 1300 hours." Marines never add the word "hours" to the end of the time. Just say meet me at 1300.

Since the time from 0100 to 1259 is the same time as 1:00 a.m. to 12:59 p.m., all you need to know is how to convert back to the regular time from 1300 to 2359. How do you know what time to meet someone at the PX if they say, "Meet me at the coffee shop at fourteen forty (1440)"?

Rather than count the hours on your fingers (which I did for many years), subtract 1200 from the time given. In our example take 1440 and subtract 1200 which equals 240 or 2:40 p.m.

Try it with the example in the first paragraph. "I will be back from the game around 1900." Take 1900, subtract 1200, and you get 700 or 7:00 p.m. Write it out a few more times, and you will sound like an old Hat* in no time.

*Hat is a nickname for drill instructor. NOTE: Your recruit should NEVER call the drill instructor a Hat!

Adapt and Overcome Action Steps:
□   Practice converting the hours of the day to military time.

Marine Corps Recruit Training Battalion Colors

During the forming phase of recruit training, recruits are placed into one of the four training battalions of the Recruit Training Regiment (RTR).

Each Recruit Training Battalion has a particular color: 1st Battalion red, 2nd Battalion gold, 3rd Battalion dark blue and 4th Battalion maroon. Each Battalion is made up of companies, and each company is made up of platoons.

The first, second and third Battalions contain four companies each. The fourth Battalion includes three companies. Each platoon has a four-digit number.

First Recruit Training Battalion (1st RTBn) is comprised of four companies: Alpha Company (A Co), Bravo (B Co), Charlie (C Co) and Delta (D Co). Each platoon (Plt) in the 1st Battalion is assigned a four-digit number starting with 1. These identifiers may be seen on the platoon's guidon (flag). For example, a recruit in 1st Battalion might be in Alpha Company, Platoon 1059.

Second Recruit Training Battalion (2nd RTBn) is comprised of four companies: Echo Company (E Co), Fox Company (F Co), Golf Company (G Co) and Hotel Company (H Co). Each platoon (Plt) in the 2nd Battalion is assigned a four-digit number starting with a 2.

Third Recruit Training Battalion (3rd RTBn) is comprised of four companies: India Company (I Co), Kilo Company (K Co), Lima Company (L Co) and Mike Company (M Co). Each platoon (Plt) in the 3rd Battalion is assigned a four-digit number starting with 3.

All of the female recruits are part of Fourth Recruit Training Battalion (4th RTBn) which is comprised of three companies: November Company (N Co), Oscar Company (O Co) and Papa Company (P Co). Each platoon (Plt) in 4th Battalion is assigned a four-digit number starting with 4.

While each training battalion has a particular color associated with it, all guidons (flags) are yellow and red and display the platoon's number.

Adapt and Overcome Action Steps:
- ☐ Look at your recruit's first letter and determine what training battalion he is in and the color for that battalion. Keep the color in mind when you order t-shirts to wear on Family Day.

Summary of Main Points:

- Your recruit cannot say more than what is in the script during the first call.
- Write encouraging, supportive letters that help your recruit stay connected to his old life.
- Battalions are divided into companies, which are then divided into platoons.
- Know which battalion, company and platoon your recruit is in.
- Each platoon has a four-digit number.

SECTION 2

Boot Camp: Everything You wanted to know but didn't know How to Ask

The Silver Hatches (photo by Vera Basilone)

Notes

CHAPTER 3

An Overview of Recruit Training

*The Values of Honor, Courage and Commitment –
imprinted on their souls during Recruit Training
and strengthened thereafter – mark a Marine's
character for a lifetime.*

*General James T. Conway
34th Commandant of the Marine Corps*

Chapter Questions:

- What is the Training Matrix?
- How can the Training Matrix help me?
- What terms do I need to know?

The Training Matrix

The Training Matrix is a calendar which arranges Marine Corps training into a schedule. These little blocks give a glimpse of a recruit's life each day. Although the calendar is a tool made for the Marines, it can help you keep track of your recruit's location and what he is doing. Keep in mind the Training Matrix is not set in stone. Commanding Officers have a little wiggle room to move things around if they need to—depending on the circumstances. For example, a DI may give a Core Value Discussion during inclement weather instead of a scheduled outdoor activity. The most recent version of the Training Matrix can be found on the Official Marine Corps website, (https://www.mcrdpi.marines.mil/Recruit-Training/Recruit-Training-Matrix/). Download a copy to your computer or print it out and follow along with me as we take a quick tour of the schedule.

Sifting Through and Making Sense of it All

I know it looks a little like a foreign language, but the Marines use acronyms and abbreviations so they can fit a lot of information in a tiny space. I recommend copying the matrix to your hard drive. This will allow you to open the document and enlarge the screen to see each block clearly, but if you don't mind the tiny characters, print off a copy to look at as you follow along.

WK	Mon	Tues	Wed	Thurs	Fri	Sat	Sun

The top left corner block reads WK, which stands for the week. Continue across the top row to see Monday through Sunday.

Processing and Forming

WK	Mon	Tues	Wed	Thurs	Fri	Sat	Sun
P	Receiving				FD1 Pick-up IST	FD2	FD3
1	FD4						

On the left side, under WK, it starts off with P, which stands for processing. The first week is their processing week, and they don't begin training yet. Monday through Thursday mark the receiving days. Those are the days new recruits arrive. On Friday—marked Pick-up, the recruits are issued uniforms and gear. Their hair is cut, and they receive a medical evaluation. They also take an Initial Strength Test (IST).

During the forming days, marked F1, F2, F3 and F4 new recruits meet their drill instructors and are "formed" into platoons.

Chapter 4 provides the details of this week.

Training Weeks

WK	MON	TUES	WED	THURS	FRI	SAT	SUN
P	RECEIVING				FD1 PICKUP IST	FD2	FD3
1	FD4	TD1 ACADEMIC CLASSES CLOSE ORDER DRILL	TD2	TD3	TD4	TD5	S1 RELIGIOUS SERVICES ACADEMIC CLASSES CVDS

The numbers 1 through 12 in the first column under P represent the training weeks. The chart is color-coded into four phases. (Each of the phases is explained in detail in chapter 5-8.)

The TD and number in each box indicates a training day. You will see 58 training days and 12 M days for a total of 70 training days. Each training day lists that days' activities. Training Day 1, for example, shows "Academic Classes and Close Order Drill." At the end of each week, the days are marked with an S, which stands for Sunday. Each Sunday, recruits may attend religious services. Training is kept at a minimum with CVD—Core Value Discussions. Sundays are not considered training days.

While these acronyms are no longer on the Training Matrix, you may come across them: L/F stands for Lead Series and Follow Series. Each company is broken down into two groups called the Lead and Follow Series. The first recruits to arrive form the first three platoons which make up the Lead Series. The next three platoons (two platoons if there are not enough recruits to make up the third one) form the Follow Series.

Adapt and Overcome Action Steps:

☐ Download your copy of the Training Matrix and continue reading for more details about each training day.

☐ Print out a copy of the Training Matrix and put it on your refrigerator, cork board, or wherever you can see it. This way you will know approximately what part of training your recruit is going through. Make an "X" in each box to mark off the days until graduation. Remember the matrix is not set in stone and will change depending upon the needs of the Marine Corps.

☐ Mention upcoming training events in a letter to offer support and show interest. Write something like, "I read next week you may be going to the swimming pool for qualification, remember the hours you spent at the pool on High Street?"

Summary of Main Points:

- The Training Matrix is a calendar you can use to keep track of what your recruit is doing each week.
- Learn the abbreviations and acronyms.
- The Training Matrix is a guideline for drill instructors. It often changes to fit the needs of the Marine Corps.
- You can use the Training Matrix to generate topics for discussion in your letters.

CHAPTER 4

Before Training Begins

Marines don't join the Marine Corps to sit on their sea bags at Camp Lejeune or Camp Pendleton. They didn't. They want to train, but they want to go somewhere and do something.

General Robert B. Neller
37th Commandant of the United States Marine Corps

Chapter Questions:
- What is receiving?
- What goes on during processing?
- What happens during forming?

Put yourself in the shoes of a new recruit for a moment. Imagine riding on a bus late in the evening. Everyone talks and tells jokes. As the bus pulls onto the causeway leading to the Parris Island front gate, you look out the window and all you see is darkness. You don't know exactly where you are and you wonder if you've made the right decision.

This chapter explores what goes on after your loved one reaches

Parris Island from the time your recruit arrives until the first day of training.

Your recruit may spend from six to ten days Receiving, Processing and Forming before any formal training begins.

Receiving

New recruits arrive via bus late at night to limit the visibility of landmarks aboard the base and disorient them. A drill instructor boards the bus and immediately starts yelling instructions. The whole experience is designed to confuse the recruits as they disembark and line up on the yellow footprints. The Receiving drill instructor gives his welcome speech giving the recruits too much information to process at one time. He will tell them to respond, "Yes, Sir!" and they will, but it won't be loud enough, or they won't understand what he just said, but they will respond with "Yes, Sir!" anyway.

On command, they will quickly walk through the silver hatches into the Receiving building to fill out paperwork after which all personal belongings are collected. At all times one or more drill instructors are either giving instructions or commanding them to move somewhere.

Next, they line up in a room with a bank of old telephones mounted in boxes to the wall. The phones make it look like they teleported back to the 1960's. One by one, they call home saying only what is written on a bullet list posted on the inside of the phone box.

After they make their call, they proceed to another classroom where they continue to fill out paperwork.

Processing

There are two processing days. During this time, recruits finish paperwork and get haircuts, or in the case of female recruits, receive instruction on authorized hairstyles for the Marine Corps. Female recruits do not get shaved heads. Haircuts are designed to make everyone look the same by erasing individuality and prior connections with civilian life. Male recruits will receive haircuts every seven to ten days throughout boot camp. Before going to the barber, Males are told to identify moles or other surface growths to avoid getting them sliced off.

Recruits get uniforms and gear issued to them and go through medical and dental evaluations. Healthy teeth are vital to a Marine, which is why there are many opportunities for recruits that need additional dental work to get it throughout boot camp. During this time they are also tested for drugs and HIV.

Before moving into their platoons, new recruits take an Initial Strength Test (IST).

If they do not pass the first time, they are moved to the Physical Rehabilitation Platoon (PRP), also called Physical Conditioning Platoon (PCP), with other recruits who do not meet weight standards or cannot pass the IST. Here they will receive remedial training until they can pass the test. If they are in the PRP or PCP, they still receive mail and would probably appreciate encouragement via letters.

The IST (initial strength test) consists of a 1.5-mile run, plank or crunches, pull-ups or push-ups.

Forming

Recruits wait until enough of them are on deck, a naval term that means the floor, to form a platoon. While they wait, they finish up any administrative tasks. Then they are "picked up" by their drill instructors and formed into a platoon. Recruits meet their drill instructors, learn about the chain of command, what is expected of them and what to do if they have any problems. They are also afforded the last opportunity to reveal any instances of fraudulent enlistment, promises made, any misconduct or any reason that may invalidate their contract. If a recruit answers "yes" to any fraudulent enlistment issues, the matter is addressed and corrective action is taken.

Adapt and Overcome Action Steps:
- ☐ Watch a video showing typical receiving activities: https://www.youtube.com/watch?v=vXwxvzvCWj4
- ☐ Subscribe to the Marines YouTube channel and search for Parris Island boot camp videos. https://www.youtube.com/channel/UCHstNaT6R-1zAOlBU_XBr_Q

Summary of Main Points:
- Three steps occur before training day 1: receiving, processing and forming.
- During receiving, new recruits find out what is expected of them.
- Processing days involve paperwork, testing and acclimation to a new way of life.
- Before heading to their new platoons, recruits are given a final chance to address fraudulent enlistment issues.

CHAPTER 5

What Goes on During Phase 1?

For over 221 years our Corps has done two things for this great Nation. We make Marines, and we win battles...

General James C. Krulak
31st Commandant of the Marine Corps

Chapter Questions:
- What happens during the first three weeks of training?
- What are Core Value Discussions and MCMAP?
- What is close order drill and what purpose does it serve in the Marine Corps?
- Why must they rappel?

Overview of the First Three Weeks

During the first phase of training, recruits leave their former life behind as they learn what is expected on a day-to-day basis, including safety procedures, care of the squad bay and basic training requirements. They are introduced to the Marine Corps Core Values: honor, courage and commitment. Drill instructors teach them discipline, fitness and esprit de corps—the corps rich tradition. The Educator's Workshop Command Brief describes esprit de corps as "the Corps' rich tradition of promoting values, instill warrior spirit and ethos and inspire enthusiasm, devotion, and pride."

Since phase one is designed to instill discipline, teach teamwork and enforce Marine Corps Standards, drill instructors use fear of the unknown coupled with confusion and stress.

As soon as the bus stops at receiving, a drill instructor boards the bus and begins the welcome to boot camp life orientation. Shouting instructive commands at the raw recruits instantly changes any preconceived reality. No matter their background each passenger is now experiencing an existence between civilian and military life. Basic survival instincts take over as the recruits re-learn how to speak, walk and think. Nothing is normal or expected at this point. This first step is a deliberate and effective method to purge singularity.

The process continues as civilian clothing is replaced by issued uniforms. Males receive identical haircuts; hairstyles for the females are limited to short, off-the-collar cuts or wound tightly into a bun. This commonality is a bonding agent between recruits. As training continues, this fear of the unknown and confusion is replaced by confidence and a sense of accomplishment. While stress may always be present, trust in their drill instructors and fellow Marine recruits ensures success.

When you look at the Training Matrix, you will notice the first three weeks are spent participating in physical training (PT); going through the confidence and obstacle courses for the first time; understanding how to use a gas mask; rappelling down a tower and learning the basics of the Marine Corps Martial Arts Program, (MCMAP). In addition, recruits attend many core value discussion (CVD), classes designed to teach them about the Marine Corps.

Week 1

Recruits attend academic classes on a variety of subjects, including an Introduction to USMC Values, USMC Ethics, Marine Corps Customs and Courtesies, the Uniform Code of Military Justice and the History and Structure of MCMAP.

Listed as martial arts on the current Training Matrix, MCMAP teaches hand to hand combat with the discipline of martial arts. These activities teach the recruits teamwork and help them gain self-esteem by pushing them to overcome unwarranted fears that keep them from accomplishing their goals.

They also get an introduction to close order drill (COD). Close order drill teaches them how to follow orders quickly and how to work as one unit.

In addition to these lessons, they participate in a 1.5-mile formation run, and they learn the proper way to throw a punch as if their lives depended on it. They take their first two courses in combat care, which includes information about first aid kits and how to tend to the wounded.

Throughout boot camp, they will continue PT and participate in Core Value Discussions (CVD). The discussions cover topics like integrity, the importance of leadership, Marine Corps values, knowing the difference between right and wrong and other subjects meant to help recruits develop their moral character.

Adapt and Overcome Action Steps:
☐ During the first week of training, recruits may ask themselves what on earth they have gotten themselves into. Write your recruit a positive letter, letting him know you support his decision to become a Marine. Send along uplifting quotes, comics, or family stories. This is a critical stage for your recruit to endure. Don't worry, the DI's will

not allow your loved one to quit, but you can be very helpful with positive support.

☐ Visit YouTube and search for USMC boot camp week 1 videos.

Week 2

During week two, recruits learn how to use pugil sticks. Pugil sticks simulate rifles with fixed bayonets. They learn fighting stances and various hand-to-hand combat techniques. For their running drill, they now run two miles rather than the 1.5 from last week.

Along with the Core Value Discussions, they also take courses in Marine Corps history; two more courses in combat care (combat care III and IV); and they learn about the rank structure and general orders. Before boot camp is over, the recruits will have to take and pass two written tests on all of the material they learned. At the end of the week, they complete a 5 km hike. Some recruits are scheduled to have dental surgery to fix problems identified during the processing phase. Training in close order drill continues.

Adapt and Overcome Action Steps:

☐ Visit YouTube and search for USMC boot camp week 2 videos

☐ Write a letter to your recruit asking him about sparing with pugil sticks. Ask about the 5 Km hike. Did your recruit do well? Did the hike challenge him? Can you think of a time your family went hiking? How do you think the recruit hike differed from a family hike?

Week 3

This week recruits go to the obstacle course and confidence course for the first time. They will return to these courses throughout boot camp.

Ten events make up the obstacle course. Instructors teach recruits how to navigate each event. Spotters standby to assist them. These obstacles test strength, stamina, balance and coordination.

The confidence course is designed to build their self-esteem by facing and conquering 15 physical tasks. It demonstrates what they can accomplish both physically and mentally, both alone and as a team. Drill instructors have the recruits warm up with exercises before beginning the course. Many of the physical tasks require considerable upper body strength and may be difficult to master. This first attempt at the confidence course serves as a baseline for the recruit. Later, recruits will attack the course again to see how much they improved.

I observed Marine instructors demonstrate each of the confidence course challenges while attending the Educator's Workshop. They made it look so easy! After attempting one or two challenges, I walked over to our Marine guide and volunteered for first aid duty. An assignment for which I am much better suited.

Recruits also visit the rappel tower, the daunting 50-foot structure, helps recruits master their fear of heights and build confidence. After retrieving gear and listening to a safety brief, recruits learn how to construct an improvised seat harness using rope and a carabiner clip. Once the harness is checked for safety, recruits rappel down the wall, which simulates a mountainside or building. Next, they ascend the tower again and rappel down the skid, a platform area without a wall. The skid simulates the landing bars on some aircraft. (Typically a helicopter).

In addition to rappelling, recruits experience the gas chamber on the same day. The building, constructed out of cement blocks and painted in a camouflage pattern, has two cream-colored doors flanked by a red sign with yellow lettering that reads, "Gas Chamber."

Outside the building Chemical, Biological, Radiological and Nuclear instructors (CBRN Instructors) go over the different types of chemical and biological weapons and how they might be used by an enemy. To ready the chamber, Marines burn o Chlorobenzylidene Malononitrile (CS) tablets, the active ingredient in a tear gas called CS gas.

Before entering the building, recruits receive an hour-long class that covers the use of the M40 Field Mask, the definition of CS gas and what to expect from the effects of the gas. Next, they enter the building wearing the masks. Once inside they go through a series of tasks designed to give them confidence that the mask works and will stay on their faces. Just after getting this assurance, they break the seal of the mask using their fingers and allow some of the CS gas to enter. Recruits follow the procedure for clearing the mask so they can breathe normally again. When directed, they exit the chamber.

During Educators' Workshop, most of the teachers volunteered to rappel. I contented myself with documenting them. The instructors coached each person on the proper way to hold the rope as they stepped off the edge. One teacher caught his glove in the carabiner, so the instructor below had to guide him down. Another teacher could not overcome her fear of heights and had to abandon her attempt, and one released too much rope and tumbled back a little before the instructor below took over. The best walked backward down the wall to the bottom without issue. The worst dangled away from the wall as the instructor lowered him to the bottom.

We also walked through the gas chamber. Marine Instructors told us the gas lingers in the building for days after being released. They kept the chamber sealed between visits so we would have the opportunity to encounter the effects, but they would not be nearly as strong as those felt by recruits who trained a few days ago. CBRN Instructors opened the doors and checked the potency of the gas residue. On command, we all walked through the door into a large space. I noticed the cement floor and a smell that reminded me of black snake fireworks. Before I made it out through the other door, my throat and eyes started burning and my nose started running. I found it hard to imagine how the recruits coped with the after-effects of the full-strength gas. The Marines told us not to touch our faces afterward lest we get traces of the gas into our eyes or irritate our skin. We walked away with a deeper understanding of what recruits go through when learning how to use their gas masks.

MCMAP training continues with classes like Armed Manipulations during which recruits learn how to block enemy strikes and keep possession of their weapon if someone tries to grab it away. They learn how to knife-fight, and they continue to work with pugil sticks. They learn chokes and offensive holds and how to counter them.

Along with their physical training, there are classes in subjects like sexual harassment, substance abuse, equal opportunity, suicide prevention, USMC History 1941–1945, History 1946–1953, and more Core Value Discussions, including one about Medal of Honor (MoH) recipient Dan Daly. Additional dental appointments are scheduled when required.

In addition to academic classes, recruits participate in an 8-mile hike and have a series commander inspection at the end of the week. The series commander along with drill instructors observe recruits' uniform appearance, bearing and confidence. They also quiz recruits on material covered in the academic classes they have taken. The inspection prepares recruits for the final commander's inspection.

Adapt and Overcome Action Steps:
☐ Visit YouTube and search for confidence course videos. Then watch recruits as they go through the course. Which tasks do you think are the most difficult? Do any of them look like they would be fun to do?

☐ Write to your recruit and ask about the different tasks. Which one did he like? Which one gave him trouble? How did he prepare for the course?

☐ Think of five questions to ask your recruit about week 3 challenges.

☐ Search YouTube for videos of recruits at the gas chamber and see what your recruit will go through as he masters the M40 field mask.

By now, you have a good idea of what your loved one is doing during Phase 1 of their training.

Summary of Main Points:
- Boot camp breaks down the individual and builds him back up as part of a team.
- Recruits continue to manage stress as they learn to rappel and use gas masks.
- MCMAP is close combat training with a Marine Corps specific martial arts component.
- Recruits visit the confidence course twice during boot camp in order to see how much they improved over time.

Notes

CHAPTER 6

What Goes on During Phase 2?

The deadliest weapon in the world is a MARINE and his rifle!

General John J. Pershing

Chapter Questions:
- What goes on each week during the second phase of boot camp?
- Why do they work so hard to learn close order drill?
- What is meant by basic water survival training?
- Where can I see graduation pictures?

Overview of the Next Four Weeks

During phase two, recruits learn marksmanship skills. They develop small unit leadership skills and how to work as a team. Also, they receive continued instruction and reinforcement of Marine Corps values.

As a period devoted to transforming recruits into Marines, their fear of the unknown and the confusion they faced during the first phase is replaced with the fear of letting their team down and not living up to the expectations of their drill instructors. Recruits continue to manage stress as they learn water survival skills training and how to shoot and qualify with a rifle on the range. They also learn basic field skills and how to lead small troop units.

Week 4 – Swim Week

The week starts with unarmed manipulations training, which is especially useful during peacekeeping or humanitarian missions. By using unarmed restraints and manipulation techniques, they learn the best way to control an aggressor without using deadly force.

Classes covering the history of the Marine Corps from the years 1976 to 2006 take place this week along with an introduction to Operational Risk Management (ORM), a course teaching the recruit how to identify hazards and minimize risk.

During swim week, recruits are not taught how to swim; they are taught basic water survival. The first event involves swimming across the shallow end of the pool without touching the bottom. They are shown and can use one of six different swim strokes to achieve this objective. If a recruit cannot pass this event, he is taken off to the side and taught how to swim on his back. After which, he will attempt the event again, and if he does not pass or he fails on another event during training, he is categorized as an Iron Duck and given extra instruction designed to make him feel comfortable around the water. Once he can swim on his back, he can continue with water survival training.

The recruits who can swim continue through the qualification process to the second event, a 25 Meter conducted self-rescue. Recruits are assisted off a 10-foot tower into the water, a move that simulates what goes one when they abandon ship. Instructors teach recruits to come up hands first to clear any kind of debris that might knock them out when they surface. Then they swim to the second silver ladder.

The third event requires staying on the surface of the water for four minutes using three different methods: treading water; lying on their back and bicycle kicking their legs, the easiest technique for weak swimmers; or inflating their blouses to make a floatation device.

The fourth event is a 25 Meter swim using waterproofed packs as a flotation device. While in the water, they are taught to use various methods to float and swim with their packs.

The final event is called the Shallow Water Gear Shed. Recruits go back to the shallow end of the pool and when directed, jump into four feet of water wearing flak jackets, Kevlar helmets, and their rifles. They tread water until given the go-ahead to submerge entirely and remove their combat equipment underwater. The instructor allows ten seconds for the recruit to remove his gear and resurface.

After successfully completing the events, recruits know how to survive and not panic while in the water with their uniforms and gear.

The week ends with a 2.5-mile run, remedial MCMAP classes if needed, MCMAP qualification and more Core Value Discussions. And, of course, there is some time allocated for dental appointments. This week recruits may also participate in a blood drive.

Adapt and Overcome Action Steps:
- ☐ Search YouTube for videos about swim week and watch the recruits as they, jump, tread water and remove combat equipment in the pool.

☐ Think of three questions to ask your recruit about swim qualification in your next letter.

Week 5 Team Week

During team week, recruits continue training, including learning how to stand post in garrison and help with various duties throughout the base. Some help pick up recycling items from the offices or sort recycling. Others help by loading trucks, moving items from one place to another, cleaning offices, washing clothing at the depot laundry, or taking care of the lawn.

If a recruit needs dental surgery to have his wisdom teeth extracted, he will go this week. After his wisdom teeth are removed, he rates one-day SIQ (sick in quarters) and one day of light duty to recuperate. Recruits must be reevaluated before they are allowed to continue training. Other recruits visit the dentist if additional dental work is required.

Recruits face many challenges this week: an initial written test, which covers Marine Corps history, drill, policies and military law; an initial drill competition, one of several competitions between platoons in the same company; a pull-up competition (PU Comp); a three-mile individual effort run (3.0 I/E Run); and a 10 Km hike. They also visit the Marine Corps Exchange, have individual photos taken and receive various inoculations.

And, of course, their learning continues with CVDs on various topics such as the Thrift Savings Plan, a retirement savings plan for active duty military and government employees.

Training for close order drill begins right away when a recruit steps into formation on the yellow footprints. It continues as the platoons march from place to place and learn how to move as one when the drill instructors call cadence. According to Marine Corps Order (MCO) 5060.20, "The object of close order drill is to teach Marines by exercise to obey orders and to do so immediately in the correct way. ... Additionally, it is still one of the finest methods for developing confidence and troop leading abilities in our subordinate leaders." Platoons in a series compete in several competitions during boot camp, one of those is close order drill. Each platoon is graded on how they perform precision drill movements. The drill instructor is also rated on the accuracy of commands.

Besides all the many challenges, individual graduation photos are taken this week by Recruit Photo on training days 26 and 27. Recruits must pay to receive copies of the picture. Most new Marines will have the photos on Family Day unless they packed them. When you receive a graduation package in the mail, it will contain order forms for graduation memorabilia. Don't worry about not having the graduation picture. The Engraving Shop and Recruit Photo work together, so there is no need to have a picture when you order banners mugs, etc. from MCCS. If later you realize there were not enough pictures to go around, you can order additional pictures from Recruit Photo, 843-228-1555.

In 2017 I interviewed a new Marine at the chow hall. He told me he enjoyed team week. He sorted recyclable items brought to the recycling center. Being away from the observant eyes of the drill instructor for a short time gave him a break from the pressures associated with constant monitoring. I experienced the watchful eyes of two drill instructors for three days and already experienced a feeling of dread every time I saw one heading my way. It must have been a great relief to get away from them if only for a short few hours a day.

Adapt and Overcome Action Steps:
- ☐ Ask your recruit if he ordered graduation photos.
- ☐ Ask your recruit where he helped out on the base during team week.
- ☐ Did your recruit have his wisdom teeth removed?

☐ Think of three questions to ask your recruit about week 5 challenges

Week 6 – Grass Week

During week 6, also called Grass Week, the recruits sit in the grass and learn how to maintain and dry fire weapons. Dry firing, also called snapping in, is simulated firing without rounds of ammunition. Recruits learn to fire their weapons in different positions: the sitting position; prone position, which is firing while lying on their stomachs; kneeling position; and standing position. In addition to dry firing, recruits take classes to learn about their weapons and safety.

As part of the 2017 Educator's Workshop, we visited the Indoor Simulated Marksmanship Trainer, (ISMT) where we practiced firing at digital targets projected on the walls. I lifted one of the rifles and marveled at the weight. It takes a good amount of arm strength to maintain a steady firing position for any length of time. Later that afternoon, we received an M16 service rifle class and fired M16s at the firing range. We wore bulky hearing protection, and the heat of the day made me tired. I remember being exhausted by the time we ate dinner, barely being able to lift my arms. And we had only a taste of what recruits do on a daily basis. My husband, Mike, showed a bit of empathy and smiled when I returned so exhausted.

Adapt and Overcome Action Steps:

☐ Has your recruit ever fired a weapon before? Ask your recruit about his experience on the rifle range. How did he shoot? Weather can influence a shooting score. How was the weather when your recruit qualified? Were the sand fleas (tiny, little, biting gnats) out that day?

Week 7 – Firing Week

During week 7, firing week, recruits practice firing their weapons with live rounds at targets. They receive scores based on the number of hits in the target scoring area. On the last day, they show their proficiency, earning an expert, sharpshooter or marksman badge based on their score. Every Marine regardless of their Military Occupational Specialty, (MOS), is a rifleman.

In addition to qualifying on the range, recruits participate in a 12 km conditioning march. They also get haircuts, learn how to maintain their clothing and equipment, take a tour of the museum, and attend more Core Value Discussions (CVD).

Adapt and Overcome Action Steps:
- ☐ Look for inspiring quotes to send to your recruit.
- ☐ Add a few newspaper articles showing scores of his favorite teams.

Summary of Main Points:
- Recruits face many physical and mental challenges during phase two.
- Recruits are not taught how to swim; they are taught basic water survival, so they do not panic while in the water with their uniforms and gear.
- In team week, they help out around the base.
- During this phase, they worry more about disappointing their drill instructors and platoon.
- In firing week, they learn how to take care of and fire their weapons.

Notes

CHAPTER 7

What Goes on During Phase 3?

The Marines fought almost solely on esprit de corps, I was certain. It was inconceivable to most Marines that they should let another Marine down, or that they could be responsible for dimming the bright reputation of their Corps. The Marines simply assumed that they were the world's best fighting men.

Robert Sherrod
American Journalist

Chapter Questions:
- What is the purpose of basic warrior training?
- Why do recruits go through the confidence course a second time?
- What is the combat fitness test?

Overview of the Next Three Weeks

Phase three is the transitionary phase where a recruit takes on more responsibility, and drill instructors become less authoritarian. Once a recruit passes the Crucible, they are no longer considered recruits, they become basically trained Marines. Drill instructors focus on sustaining this transition. They do this by gradually moving from a disciplinarian to a mentor. Recruits go through basic warrior training, learn land navigation skills, and complete the second run through the confidence course. Final tests are given for combat fitness and MCMAP. They take a final PFT, a final written test, participate in a final drill competition and undergo the Crucible. Before the end of testing week, recruits stand the Company Commander's Inspection. Core Value Discussions continue with topics like financial responsibility, sexual responsibility, domestic violence/child abuse, ethics and combat leadership.

Week 8 – Basic Warrior Training

Recruits begin basic warrior training (BWT) this week: first with classroom instruction in basic field skills; and then with field experience, crawling in the sand and under barbed wire. The exercises promotes teamwork and teaches them how to keep moving when fired upon. They learn about improvised explosive devices (IEDs), what they are and how to detect them and how to navigate using a compass and a map. They also practice giving commands using verbal and non-verbal cues. On the weekend, they attend more CVD's.

Adapt and Overcome Action Steps:
- ☐ Did your recruit know how to use a map and compass before boot camp? When you write your next letter, ask your recruit what he learned during land navigation classes.
- ☐ Read the article on BWT, then think of three additional questions to ask in your next letter. https://www.parrisisland.com/1065/pi023-recruits-learn-combat-basics-on-parris-island/

Week 9

This week recruits continue with academic classes and physical training. Those proficient in another language take a foreign language test. They will visit the tailor to have their dress and service uniforms fitted and take their final combat fitness test (CFT).

Before the week is over, they will stand their Company Commander's Inspection and participate in more Core Value Discussions. At the end of the week, they will relocate to Weapons and Field Training Battalion, (WFTB). There they will continue with field skills such as field sanitation, camouflage/cover/conceal (Cam/Cvr/Conceal) and building field exercise shelters.

Recruits take practical application evaluations, the combat fitness test (CFT) and complete their second run through the confidence course. After eight weeks of training, they have more upper body strength, making the obstacles easier to achieve than the first time, thereby, giving them more confidence.

According to Captain Branden Koonce in a DOD combat fitness test video, "The combat fitness test measures endurance and physical strength as it pertains to combat-related events. Recruits simulate ammo resupply by doing ammo can presses; they do low crawls and high crawls to simulate maneuver under fire; and they implement fireman carries to simulate casualty evacuations."

Adapt and Overcome Action Steps:
- [ ] If your recruit is proficient in another language, how did he do during the foreign language test?
- [ ] How did he do on the Company Commander's Inspection?
- [ ] Next week is the Crucible. Some family members make or buy a special candle which they light during the demanding 54-hour event. If you would like to participate in this tradition, you can burn regular votive candles or get creative and make your own crucible candle. Online shops sell

candles decorated with a Marine motif. Search for "Crucible candle" on the internet and view images of what other people have done in the past. Just remember to be careful where you burn your candle. Make sure to keep it away from anything flammable and do not leave it unattended.

Week 10 – Final Testing and Crucible

Recruits take their final physical fitness Test (PFT), final written exam and final drill evaluation. This week they transition from recruit to Marine as they undergo the 54 hour Crucible, described in the 2017 Educators Workshop Command Brief as "a field training event, executed at the end of recruit training that evaluates a recruit's mental, moral and physical development in order to validate the transformation into a United States Marine." When they complete the Crucible, which ends in a 9-mile hike, they earn their Eagle Globe and Anchor (EGA). After the Crucible and EGA Ceremony, they sit down to a well-deserved hot meal at the chow hall. Unlike a normal recruit breakfast, this warrior's breakfast includes steak, as much food as they want and more time to eat.

Notice the overlap from Phase 3 to Phase 4. Once recruits transition to Marines, they enter Phase 4, called Marine Training Days.

Adapt and Overcome Action Steps:
- ☐ Double check the graduation day for your recruit. If you decided to try to get a room on the base, make a note to call the Osprey Inn on Parris Island to reserve a room 15 days in advance of the graduation date. Let the reservation desk know you are coming to see your recruit graduate.
- ☐ If you bought or made a crucible candle, set it up as a reminder of your loved one's challenge this week. **WARNING:** Do not leave burning candles unattended and keep them away from anything flammable.

☐ Watch this video about the Crucible to get an idea of what goes on during this event.
https://www.youtube.com/watch?v=ikSHI7RxyCM

Summary of Main Points:
- During phase three, recruits take all their written and physical tests.
- The last test is a 54-hour long crucible.
- At the end of this phase, they graduate from a recruit to a basically trained Marine.

Notes

CHAPTER 8

What Goes on During Phase 4?

Every Marine is, first and foremost, a rifleman. All other conditions are secondary.

General Alfred M. Gray
29th Commandant of the Marine Corps

Chapter Questions:
- What is the purpose of the 4th Phase?
- Why are they called Marine training days?
- What goes on during Marine Phase

Overview of the Last Two Weeks

The last two weeks of training focus on Marine to Marine mentoring and leadership development. General Robert B. Neller, 37th Commandant of the Marine Corps said, "...Now they (drill instructors) have another few days to talk to their new Marines as a fellow Marine about what it is going to be like as they get ready to go out and begin the rest of their journey as a Marine."

Drill instructors and senior drill instructors continue to mentor new Marines by providing "squad talks, platoon talks, Marine panels and warfighting discussions; all focused on mentoring new Marines and preparing them to be ethical warriors," according to the Parris Island Office of Communication Strategy and Operations.

Week 11

The first Marine training day, (M1), begins on the last day of the Crucible. During week 11, drill instructors and senior drill instructors continue to mentor new Marines by providing squad leadership discussions covering topics such as marriage, domestic violence, driver's safety and financial responsibility.

Five Force Fitness sessions take place throughout the week. Captain Flores, Director, Office of Communication for Parris Island, describes these as classes that "incorporate regenerative physical training sessions such as yoga and various low-intensity movements to help with recovery from the Crucible/training cycle." These sessions also teach new Marines how to maintain physical fitness throughout their careers.

In a class called Marine Panels, new Marines are separated into groups by MOS. Experienced Marines from the same field give new Marines "insight as to what their jobs in the fleet will entail, what to expect at their MOS school and how best to prepare to be successful in their future service within the Marine Corps," according to Captain Flores.

Time is allocated to take Platoon photos, turn in equipment, pick-up personal items and make travel arrangements.

Chief drill instructors and above lead platoon leadership discussions and cover topics like fraternization, sexual responsibility, social media and leader development.

They also receive briefs about the services and resources available to them from MCCS, Navy Marine Corps Relief Society and the Red Cross. At the end of the week, they enjoy base liberty.

Week 12 – Graduation Week

New Marines use this week to finish administrative tasks; return their weapons; pick up pictures and uniforms; pay bills; practice for graduation; participate in the motivational run; and attend Family Day.

They even squeeze in few more Core Value Discussion classes. Time is also allocated for briefs about the School of Infantry, (SOI) and Marine Combat Training, (MCT). The Graduation Ceremony is the last day of boot camp.

Adapt and Overcome Action Steps:

- ☐ If you are driving to Parris Island, get some glass chalk and decorate your vehicle windows for your new Marine. Make sure you do not obstruct the view of the driver.
- ☐ Some families buy banners to hold during the moto run. These can be ordered on the internet and vary in price. Order early, so you have it in time.
- ☐ If your new Marine is coming home with you, make or buy a banner welcoming him home. Hang it up before you leave to pick-up your new Marine or designate a family member to hang it up before you arrive home. My husband had a "Welcome Home" banner waiting for him. He still remembers it.
- ☐ After graduation view or print extra copies of your Marine's Graduation program. https://www.mcrdpi.marines.mil/Resources/Graduation-Info/Graduation-Program/

Summary of Main Points:
- By phase 4 your recruit is a basically trained Marine.
- Phase 4 helps new Marines understand what to expect as they move on from basic training into their MOS and beyond.
- New Marines attend panels, briefs and classes given by Marines established in their careers. These Marines offer guidance and answer questions.
- Drill instructors continue their role as mentors.

SECTION 3

Getting Ready for Graduation

Graduation Day (photo by Vera Basilone)

Notes

CHAPTER 9

Getting Ready to Visit Parris Island, South Carolina

Old breed? New breed? There's not a damn bit of difference so long as it's the Marine breed.

General Chesty Puller

Chapter Questions:
- How do I sign up for graduation events?
- What goes on during the command reception with depot leadership?
- How many people can attend the graduation?
- Are there places to stay on Parris Island?
- What should I take on the trip?

First Things First

As soon as you find out what day your loved one is scheduled to graduate from Boot camp, visit the graduation week activities and events page on the Marine Corps Community Services' (MCCS) web site. There you can sign up for graduation week e-mail notifications regarding any Family Day changes, updates, or cancellations.

Next head over to the EventBrite page (links for these sites are in the Action Steps) and sign up for any Family Orientation Day and Family Liberty Day activities you wish to attend. Some events are free, others have a cost. Chapter 9 will go into greater detail about the activities and include an itinerary of each day.

Command Reception with Depot Leadership

On EventBrite you can sign up for dinner with base leaders. Your new Marine cannot attend, but meeting with Marine officers, drill instructors and other active duty Marines will provide you with a unique opportunity to ask questions about the Marine Corps. You may even meet the Commanding General of Parris Island, if he is available. Current Marines will share their experiences with you and let you know what comes next. I recommend attending. The knowledge you gain from speaking with Marines about their experiences in the Corps will help you understand more about what your loved one went through in boot camp and more about the Marine Corps lifestyle. If you prefer, you can always eat out in town instead.

Adapt and Overcome Action Steps:

- ☐ Go to the MCRD Parris Island Graduation Week Activities and Events page. http://www.mccs-sc.com/mil-fam/recruit/index.shtml
  Make sure you sign up for the e-mails they send out the week of graduation. These e-mails will contain information about Family Day changes, updates, or cancellations.
- ☐ Next view the EventBrite MCRD Parris Island Graduation Week Activities & Events sign up page. https://www.eventbrite.com/o/mcrd-parris-island-graduation-week-activities-amp-events-1920813227

- ☐ If you wish, sign up for the Family Day Dinner with the Depot Command.
- ☐ If the events are sold out contact MCCS at 843-228-1667 or e-mail them at recruitfamilies@usmc-mccs.org to see if they can accommodate you.
- ☐ Make a list of questions you have about life in the Marine Corps and take it with you to the dinner.

Who can visit?

At one time there were no restrictions on the number of guests allowed to attend a graduation. Unfortunately, the Marine Corps stopped in person graduations on Parris Island in 2020 due to the Covid19 pandemic. Starting May 7, 2021, Parris Island will gradually reopen to visitors depending upon conditions. Check the Recruit Family Facebook page for updates and additional requirements before making plans to attend a graduation.

To drive a vehicle onto Parris Island, you will need the following:
1) A valid driver's license
2) Vehicle registration
3) Proof of auto insurance

If you are driving a rental car, you will need a valid driver's license, proof of liability insurance and a copy of your rental agreement. In addition to the proper documentation, motorcycle riders must wear protective clothing including a helmet or they will not be permitted on the base. Keep in mind you are subject to search. Do not attempt to enter Parris Island while transporting weapons. Visit the Official Marine Corps website for more information: http://www.mcrdpi.marines.mil/Visitors/FAQ/#q8

There are many options for hotels and places to stay in the Beaufort, South Carolina area. You may wish to stay farther away in Bluffton or Hilton Head. Once you know you loved one's graduation day, search the internet to find hotels near Parris Island and see which ones fit your needs. Make sure to book hotels out in town as soon as possible. Remember to find out how to cancel without penalty in case your plans change.

Lodging Options on Parris Island

The Osprey Inn

There is only one hotel located on Parris Island. And like all other options, there are advantages and disadvantages to staying there.

The main advantage for the Osprey Inn is the location. It is on Parris Island, right off the main road, Blvd. de France. Another advantage is you can walk to most of the Family Day and Graduation Day events. You won't have to worry about driving around, finding a place to park, or fighting traffic to get on base for Family Day and Graduation Day. The Inn is close to the Douglas Visitors' Center, Parade Deck, Tram and the Headquarters building, location of the Colors Ceremony.

Perhaps, the best advantage of staying at the Osprey Inn is you have a room close by to take your new Marine on Family Day when he is not allowed to leave the base. Rather than walk around Parris Island the whole time where the pressure is on for your Marine to look his best for everyone, he can relax in privacy with you in the hotel room! You can stock it with food and drinks you know your new Marine will like and the microwave is perfect for reheating a favorite lunch or snack. You can also invite other family members back to the room.

However, the Osprey Inn does not accept reservations until 15 days before your loved one's graduation date. Rooms are on a space-available basis. If you wait that long to book a hotel and the Osprey Inn is full, it will be difficult to book a hotel out in town. Additionally, you can be bumped from your room by a Marine who needs the space up to 24 hours before your stay. With this in mind, the best course of action is to book a hotel out in town as early as possible. Then write down the dates you can cancel without penalty. Cancel out in town reservations only when you are sure you can stay on base.

The rooms are not luxury rooms. They are clean and utilitarian, but if you want something fancy, you should get a room at one of the finer hotels off base. Just remember your new Marine cannot leave the base on Family Day.

Adapt and Overcome Action Steps:
- ☐ Search the Internet and look at some of the hotels in the area.
- ☐ Look at hotel's cancellation policies. Look at reviews on Trip Advisor to read what other people have to say about local accommodations.
- ☐ Book a hotel as soon as you know your loved one's graduation date and jot down the last day to cancel without penalty in case your plans change.

Parris Island RV Park

Rather than stay in a hotel, consider driving your RV and setting up camp at the RV Park located on the base. It's open year-round to a variety of patrons including guests of graduating Marines who may rent a space at the RV Park during graduation week. Call 843-228-7472 for the most current rates. New Marines probably want to go right home after they graduate, so staying on base after the graduation is not a good idea. But if you get here a day before Family Day, you can spend the time familiarizing yourself with the base.

The park has 18 large lots with water, sewer, electrical hook up and picnic tables. There are restrooms, showers, coin-operated washers, dryers and P.O. Boxes available. Water, sewer, electrical hookup and

Wi-Fi are included in the fee.

Staying on the base has its advantages. The beach is right down the road; and the Parris Island Museum, Peatross Parade Deck and the Douglas Visitors' Center are only a mile or two away. If you bring your golf clubs, you can play a round of golf at the Legends Golf Course only two miles down the road.

Need groceries? If you are a qualified patron with a valid ID, you can shop at the Commissary; if not, stop at the Food Lion grocery store on Parris Island Gateway right outside the base. Bring your grill and have a cookout. If you have a fishing license for South Carolina, you can fish at Elliott's beach and catch your dinner.

With the RV Park only a few miles from the Peatross Parade Deck, you won't have to get up at 0300 (3 a.m.) to make it to Family Day and Graduation Day activities on time. Imagine getting a good night's sleep, then waking up with plenty of time to have breakfast before heading over to the Douglas Visitors' Center. Also, this is a great place to have family and friends meet. Like the Osprey Inn, it can serve as a quiet haven for your new Marine on Family Day.

To make reservations at the RV Park, call 843-228-7472 Monday through Saturday from 0800 to 1630 (8 a.m. to 4:30 p.m.); the office is closed Sundays and Federal Holidays. Make your reservations at least five business days before your visit. Verify check-in/check-out times which are currently 1400 (2 p.m.) check-in and 1100 (11:00 a.m.) check-out. You must make reservations in the name of your new Marine unless you are a qualified patron, then you can make the reservations in your own name.

You can drive your RV around the base, but you won't be able to park it just anywhere. If you park in an unauthorized area, you will be required to move. Remember to be respectful to base personnel. If you are asked to move the vehicle to another location, please move it. Being on base is a privilege, not a right. If you can, bring a smaller means of transportation along so you can drive it around the base. If not, park your RV in the designated parking lot by the parade deck and take the tram or walk.

Adapt and Overcome Action Steps
- ☐ Visit http://www.mccs-sc.com/din-lod/rvpark.shtml for additional information to see if the RV Park is the right option for you and your family.
- ☐ Search online for RV parks around Beaufort if you are interested in parking your RV off base.
- ☐ Make sure to write down the last day to cancel in case your plans change.

What to pack

In addition to comfortable seasonal clothing for the drive down and back, bring a business casual outfit for the graduation. Most people bring something they might wear to church.

For Family Day, wear battalion t-shirts with your loved one's battalion colors. You can order them online or purchase them when you arrive in Beaufort.

Pack any medicines you need and make sure all prescription medication is in its original labeled container if you intend to bring it onto the base. Military Police are authorized to go through personal property, and you will be subject to search before entering the graduation area.

Have a good video camera and a camera for stills so you can take lots and lots of good pictures to share with other family members. Some people even made videos of their trip to Parris Island to show their new Marines. If you don't have a dedicated camera, use your smartphone to take still pictures and video. Then share graduation moments with loved ones who cannot attend.

Buy some liquid chalk markers to decorate your car windows. Your new Marine will love seeing "Proud Family of a new Marine" written on your back window. Be mindful and do not obstruct the driver's view.

Insect repellent is a must, especially in the warmer weather months. Take sunscreen and perhaps a hat to shield your head. The sun can be intense while you are walking around the base. During the summer months, we get pop-up showers, and you never know when it might rain, so stash an umbrella in the car just in case.

Bring quarters and shiny pennies for the penny presses on base. For 51 cents you can have a penny pressed with one of the images of Parris Island as an inexpensive reminder of your trip.

You may wish to bring a pair of binoculars to zoom in on your new Marine during formation.

Adapt and Overcome Action Steps:
- ☐ The National Weather Service will give you the forecast for Beaufort, South Carolina. Bookmark the page so you can return to it closer to graduation. They have a seven-day forecast, so you can see what the weather will be like before you visit. http://forecast.weather.gov/MapClick.php?lat=32.3495&lon=-80.6775#.WiAxzFWnHIU
- ☐ Make a list of all of the things you need.
- ☐ Check items off the list as you pack.

Inclement Weather

When hurricanes or other bad weather conditions threaten the area, the base Command will make a decision about the graduation and whether or not to evacuate recruits and base personnel. Sometimes they have the graduation a day early, sometimes they change the time or the venue depending on weather conditions. Make sure you bookmark the MCCS webpage and follow the Official Parris Island Facebook page for additional information. These are the places you will find information about any changes in the place, date or time of a graduation.

Adapt and Overcome Action Steps:
- ☐ Bookmark the MCCS web page: http://www.mccs-sc.com/mil-fam/recruit/index.shtml
- ☐ Follow the Official Parris Island Facebook page: https://www.facebook.com/ParrisIsland/

Summary of Main Points:
- There are various options of where to stay on base and off.
- Make sure to do your research and find out their cancellation policy
- Pack all the necessary items, bring items to support your Marine —a shirt in his battalion's color, chalk to decorate your car, pennies for the machine and a good camera.
- Be sure to bookmark the MCCS webpage and follow the Official Parris Island Facebook page to receive information about any changes for the graduation.

Notes

CHAPTER 10

Family Day

We are United States Marines, and for two and a quarter centuries we have defined the standards of courage, esprit and military prowess.

General James L. Jones
32nd Commandant of the Marine Corps

Chapter Questions:
- How do I get onto the base?
- Are there any advantages to arriving on Wednesday?
- What goes on during Family Day?

Getting onto Parris Island

Make sure to arrive early! Allow yourself at least 45 minutes to get from the Parris Island Causeway (a long strip of road leading to the front gate) to your destination. On Family Day, traffic is diverted at 0645 (6:45 a.m.) when Blvd de France closes in preparation for the motivational run. If you do not park before that time, you will find yourself hunting for a parking spot farther away from the event. One family told me they missed the Moto Run as they drove around the back streets looking for a parking space.

Two roads lead to Parris Island: Parris Island Gateway and Ribaut

Road. After taking the Parris Island exit, these roads intersect. Vehicles arriving from Parris Island Gateway must yield to those driving in from Ribaut Road. If you are on the Parris Island Gateway side, use caution as those approaching from Ribaut Road often speed through without regard to those who are merging. On Family Day, the extra traffic may cause a backup from the Parris Island Gateway side.

Next, you will notice an empty guard shack (the old front entrance). Stop here only if the electric billboard or a traffic officer directs you to do so. The billboard is located to the right of the checkpoint and may display a message. The message changes so make sure to read it and give yourself extra time to navigate any alterations to traffic patterns.

About a mile down the road, you will cross Archer's Creek. Signs will instruct you to reduce your speed. Where more lanes appear, move to the far right lane leading to the inspection area.

A pass is not necessary to get onto the base for Family Day and Graduation. However, you are required to have proper identification, which includes a valid driver's license, proof of insurance and vehicle registration. It is not clear why vehicle passes are still sent out by individual battalions, but at the time of this writing, they are not needed.

After you go through the inspection area, turn left and then right to enter the traffic circle. A sign will prompt you to take the second exit for Family Day events. When you arrive, park at the lot by the Peatross Parade deck unless otherwise instructed.

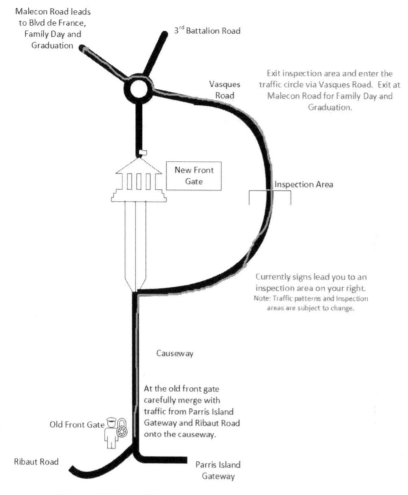

Malecon Road leads to Blvd de France, Family Day and Graduation

3rd Battalion Road

Vasques Road

Exit inspection area and enter the traffic circle via Vasques Road. Exit at Malecon Road for Family Day and Graduation.

New Front Gate

Inspection Area

Currently signs lead you to an inspection area on your right.
Note: Traffic patterns and inspection areas are subject to change.

Causeway

At the old front gate carefully merge with traffic from Parris Island Gateway and Ribaut Road onto the causeway.

Old Front Gate

Ribaut Road

Parris Island Gateway

Diagram of visitor traffic pattern. Not to scale. Drawing by Vera Basilone

What You Can and Cannot Bring Onto the Base:

Allowed:

1. Leashed pets are allowed on the base but they are restricted from many areas on base*

2. Food and coolers may be enjoyed in designated picnic areas.

3. Prescription Drugs are allowed but must be in their original labeled containers

Not Allowed:

1. Firearms or weapons

2. Illegal drugs or drug paraphernalia

3. Food on the Peatross Parade Deck

* Dogs may not attend any military ceremonies nor are they permitted in the temporary lodging facilities. Also, they are restricted from medical facilities, public facilities and any place that serves food.
** Guide dogs are an exception to these rules. Visit: http://www.mcrdpi.marines.mil/Visitors/FAQ/#q27, for additional information.

Adapt and Overcome Action Steps:
- ☐ Take a look at the Parris Island map to familiarize yourself with the entrance onto the base.

Is there any Advantage to Arriving on Wednesday Instead of Thursday?

If you arrive on Thursday, you will save money for one night at a hotel, but you will miss out on the behind-the-scenes tour as well as the time you can spend getting familiar with the base.

Advantages

- If you arrive the day before Family Day, you can orient yourself to the base by locating the points of interest as you drive or walk around.

- You can watch recruits train.

- You can do some shopping at the Marine Corps Exchange. Family members can purchase food and items from the souvenir section like t-shirts, mugs and other USMC gifts without a sponsor.

- Check-in Wednesday at the Douglas Visitors' Center and beat the Family Day crowd. You need only check in once, so no need to check in again on Thursday. Since the tram does not go everywhere, there is a lot of walking required on Family Day. If a family member needs a wheelchair, you may wish to bring one with you. The Douglas Visitors' Center has some wheelchairs available on a first come first served basis.

- You could attend the Marine Corps 101 Brief at the Douglas Visitors' Center including a behind-the-scenes tour if you signed up for it in advance. If you didn't sign up for it, ask if they have any open seats; they may be able to accommodate you. MCCS gives the 101 Brief on Thursday, but they do not include the behind the scenes tour.

- At 1330, (1:30 p.m.) you can attend the Family Orientation Brief.

- The base restaurant, Traditions, has a steak night from 1700 to 2000, (5:00 p.m. to 8:00 p.m.) There is a cost associated with dinner and reservations are required. You can also eat somewhere out in town if you like.

Disadvantages

- You will probably not see your new Marine today.
- If you decide to visit the Marine Corps Exchange (MCX) on Wednesday, and you or someone with you is not an authorized patron (active-duty Marine, other active-duty service member, Armed Forces retirees, dependents, and

reservists) you will be allowed to purchase only souvenirs and sundries.

- Your Marine will not be present at any of the day's events as he will be preparing for graduation.

Adapt and Overcome Action Steps:
☐ Make a list of pros and cons to decide if arriving on Wednesday is the right course of action for you and your family members.

Who can shop at the MCX?

Family members can purchase food in the MCX and items from the souvenir section. You can also buy gasoline at the Exchange. Anything else, including cigarettes and alcohol, must be acquired by an authorized patron. Authorized patrons are active-duty military personnel, military dependents, reservists and military retirees.

Family Day

Get there early and check in at the Douglas Visitors' Center. The Visitor's Center opens at 0600 (6:00 a.m.) After you check-in, browse the shopping area. When I looked, they had red stadium seat cushions with an Eagle Globe and Anchor (EGA) printed on them—a great item to keep your tushy comfy on the hard stadium seats. Java Café opens early too so you can grab some coffee before heading outside to find a place to view the motivational run.

Motivational Run

Your new Marine will run with all of the graduates along a pre-designated route starting and ending at the Peatross Parade Deck.

Get there as early as possible and find a good place to stand or sit. In order to see and cheer the Marines on as they run by the crowd, find a spot on either side of Blvd de France by the parade deck. It will take a little while to complete the run so make sure you are comfortable. If you purchased a banner, this is a great place to break it out and hold it up high as the new Marines run by the crowd. I saw some fabulous signs when I visited in March. One banner stood out, so I asked the family if it was expensive. They said they paid about $150 for it. You can buy a less expensive banner from MCCS, (the order form will be in your graduation packet), or make one yourself but just know many companies will make a customized banner as fancy as your wallet will allow.

The run takes place beginning and ending at the Peatross Parade Deck around 0700 or 0715 (7:00 a.m. or 7:15 a.m.) depending upon when the sun rises.

Adapt and Overcome Action Steps:
- ☐ Arrive on base early to get ready for the motivational run.
- ☐ Make the Douglas Visitors' Center your first stop. Check in, get maps, get some information and view the tram schedule.
- ☐ Before you leave the Douglas Visitors' Center, confirm the location of Friday's graduation, (e.g., will it be at the All Weather Training Facility (AWTF) because of inclement weather, the Peatross Parade Deck, or somewhere else?)

Parris Island Museum

The Parris Island Museum, the first Marine Corps command museum, opened on January 8, 1975. Give yourself some time to explore the 10,000 sq. ft. facility. While you are there, you will experience going back in time, before the base belonged to the Marine Corps, and then flash forward to the history of the base as a Marine Corps Recruit Depot. You will view images and displays depicting Marines throughout the years. You can also explore the history of recruit training and the role of women in the Marine Corps.

The museum is open every day from 1000 to 1630 (10:00 a.m. to 4:30 p.m.) except for New Year's, Easter, Thanksgiving and Christmas. On Family Day and Graduation Days, they open at 0800 (8:00 a.m.). There is no charge for admission, although they will accept donations. Since recruits visit the museum as part of their training, you may wish to go before Family Day. You can also pop in on Family Day between events or after base liberty ends at 1500 (3:00 p.m.), for your new Marine. The museum also has a gift shop with unique Marine items. Visit their online store too. Your purchases will help support the Parris Island Museum and its mission of education and preservation.

Adapt and Overcome Action Steps:
- ☐ Allow extra time to tour the museum while you are on the base. It is worth your time.
- ☐ Find the penny press machine at the museum and have your coin pressed into a reminder of your visit.
- ☐ Pick up an Iron Mike driving tour map at the museum and see other places around the base at your leisure.

Marine Corps 101 Brief at the Douglas Visitors' Center

If you did not attend the Marine Corps 101 Brief on Wednesday, you have another opportunity to go on Thursday from 0800 to 0900, (8:00 a.m. to 9:00 a.m.). You must sign up in advance for this event. If you already attended the brief on Wednesday, you have roughly one and a half hours before the Liberty Ceremony begins at the All Weather Training Facility (AWTF). You can use this time to visit the museum, get a bite to eat, or visit the Marine Corps Exchange. Just remember to give yourself plenty of time to get to the AWTF early to find a good seat.

Battalion Commander's Brief to Families & Liberty Ceremony

Arrive a little early for the brief, which begins at 0930 (9:30 a.m.) and find a seat in the All Weather Training Facility. If you are allowed to choose your seats, sit as close to the deck (floor) as possible so that you can get to your new Marine faster. This is the moment you've been waiting for! When the ceremony ends, your new Marine will be on base liberty until 1500 (3:00 p.m.). After you make your way through the crowd to find your new Marine, he will want to show you what he did during training. Let him be your guide and have fun touring the base. Remember to take lots of photos and video and always watch out for traffic!

Lunch

Your new Marine will not be allowed to leave the base, but you will have several options open to you. Visit ParrisIsland.com, eating on base for ideas. You can also order a picnic lunch or pizzas through EventBrite. I have heard the food is good, but it might not be enough to satisfy the hunger of your new Marine. And there is always a chance your Marine may want to eat something else, like a burger from Bricks or a sandwich from Subway. Traditions Restaurant also offers an all-you-can-eat buffet style meal, which includes your drink and dessert. No reservations are necessary for lunch.

Warrior's Prayer at the Recruit Chapel

At 14:00 (2:00 p.m.) visit the chapel for the warrior's prayer and marvel at the unique stained glass windows. Some have a military theme and others a biblical theme. Many were donated by various Marine Corps organizations.

Liberty Ends

At 15:00 (3:00 p.m.) base liberty ends for your new Marine, but that doesn't mean you have to leave the base right away. If you are attending the Command Reception at 16:00 (4:00 p.m.), you have an hour before it starts. If you are not attending the Command Reception, there is plenty of time to fit in one or more of the activities listed below.

Adapt and Overcome Action Steps:
- ☐ Look at the Iron Mike driving tour map and tour the base at your own pace.
- ☐ Head back to the museum and explore the history of the Marine Corps.
- ☐ Stop by the Brig and Brew, a sports bar and recreational area located on Santo Domingo Street in Building 19. You'll find plenty of parking in the parking lot across the street by the swimming pool. Inside there are pool tables, TV's, darts and a very nice bar. Visit http://www.mccs-sc.com/rec-fit/brignbrew.shtml for current Brig and Brew hours.
- ☐ Stop by the Peatross Parade Deck to watch new Marines practice for graduation.

Command Reception with Depot Command Members

The Command Reception begins at 16:00 (4:00 p.m.) at Traditions, Building 78 on Nicaragua St. instead of the Lyceum which was damaged during Hurricane Matthew in 2016. If you decide to attend the event, you will get to meet some of the officers in charge of base operations. Dinner begins after the General's welcome remarks. While you dine, you will have the opportunity to ask questions, speak with other family members and meet some Marines. You must register for this event and pay for tickets before attending.

After dinner, relax then turn in early. Tomorrow is graduation day!

Summary of Main Points:
- Allow plenty of time to get onto the base and find parking.
- Decide whether arriving a day before Family Day is best for you.
- Bring a banner and wear your new Marine's battalion colors on Family Day.

- Consider attending the Command Reception and dinner where you will have the chance to meet with other family members and ask questions.

Notes

CHAPTER 11

Customs and Courtesies
How to Act on Base

The United States Marine Corps, perhaps more than any other military organization in the world, prides itself on processing all that is high in military efficiency and soldierly qualities.

A Brief History of the United States Marine Corps

Chapter Questions:
- Are there special rules to follow when I am on base?
- Can I speak with Marines when they are in formation?
- How do I address the Marines I meet?

Driving on Base

Driving on base can be demanding, especially on Family Day. By following the tips below you can minimize stress and make the day enjoyable for you and those around you.

Signs

When you take the exit for Parris Island, you will see an unmanned post. This building is the guard shack for the old front gate. The main gate has been relocated, but the remnants of the old guard shack remain. There will be a digital sign welcoming you to Parris Island. Continue onto the causeway. I know it is tempting, but do not stop. If you stop, traffic backs up. Other signs along the way will guide you to parking or let you know if an area is off limits. As you continue toward the front gate, notice the posted speed limit signs and slow down when required.

Obey all speed signs. If the sign reads 45 MPH, drive 45 miles an hour. There are few things more frustrating than being behind someone going 25 MPH in a 45 MPH zone, especially while driving to work! If you are lost or would like to stop and observe a monument, watch troops as they march down the sidewalk, or view the statue of Iron Mike, please pull over and allow traffic to pass. Never stop in the middle of the road to enjoy the view, take a picture, or chat with someone.

Do not use your hand held cell phone while driving and do not text! It's dangerous and distracting. There are lots of visitors and permanent personnel on the base running around during the day. If you are not paying attention while driving, you could hit someone. If you get a phone call, pull over and then answer it or use a hands-free device.

Walking on Parris Island

When walking around the base, please use crosswalks and do not step out into the road until you are ready to cross. Vehicles aboard the depot stop for pedestrians in the crosswalk. If you step off the road and just stand there, drivers will not know whether to stop or continue on their way.

If you see Marines or recruits in formation, do not walk over or talk to them. Do not shout out to your new Marine. And do not make contact with recruits who are training.

If you are walking around during morning colors, when the U.S. Flag is raised, or evening colors, when the U.S. flag is lowered for the day, stop walking, stand if you are sitting, face the flag and wait until the music stops playing. If you are in your vehicle, pull over and wait until the music stops playing.

Do not walk on the Parade Deck during the Graduation Ceremony. Wait until after the troops are dismissed before going to your new Marine.

How to Speak with Marines

You may address Marines in uniform by their rank and last name. If you are unsure of their rank, it is always polite to use sir or ma'am.

Adapt and Overcome Action Steps
☐   Take a look at the rank structure http://www.marines.mil/Marines/Ranks.aspx, and brush up on the difference between a Sgt. and a GySgt.

Summary of Main Points:
- Pay attention and observe the signs.
- Do not disturb Marines in formation.
- Respect the morning and evening colors during the music.

Notes

CHAPTER 12

Points of Interest

The Marines I have seen around the world have the cleanest bodies, the filthiest minds, the highest morale and the lowest morals of any group of animals I have ever seen. Thank God for the United States Marine Corps!

Eleanor Roosevelt

Chapter Question:
- What places should I visit while on the Depot?

Parris Island has a long history dating back to the 1500's when French and Spanish explorers tried to establish forts in the vicinity of the Legends golf course. These settlements were eventually abandoned until the English took control of the Island and set up the first permanent colony. The museum has plenty of information if you would like to know more.

There are many places of interest you will want to check out:

4th Battalion

The 4th Battalion Complex is where all female recruits are trained. Their male counterparts are trained at either MCRD San Diego or MCRD Parris Island. Way back in 1949, female recruits were billeted in Building 902, current site of 6th District Headquarters. In February 1975, female recruits moved into the WM Complex you see today.

All Weather Training Facility (AWTF)

Located on Blvd de France, just past the parking lot from the Peatross Parade Deck, the AWTF is where you will pick up your new Marine after the Liberty Ceremony on Family Day. This facility is also used for graduations during inclement weather and other ceremonies throughout the year.

ATM Locations

There are ATMs located around the base. One is outside the Marine Corps Exchange (MCX), one by the Post Office and FSN bank, one in the Douglas Visitors' Center/Java Café, one inside the front door of the Commissary and one at the Navy Federal Credit Union.

Brig and Brew

The Brig and Brew bar is located in Building 19 on Santo Domingo Street. Repurposed years ago from a Brig to a sports bar, Brig and Brew is a great place to stop for a beer or a mixed drink and a snack. My husband and I stop by every now and then after work to see our friends and solve all world problems.

To locate the Brig and Brew, drive down Blvd. de France and make a left on N. Santa Domingo Street by Iron Mike. About a block down on your right, you will see the sign Brig and Brew. Park in the lot across the street.

Charlesfort- Santa Elena National Historic Landmark

If you are a bit of a history buff and would like to know more about the first settlers on Parris Island, visit the Charlesfort-Santa Elena National Historic Landmark located near The Sand Trap Grill, building 299. At different times during the 1500's, both the French and Spanish attempted to establish a foothold in the area but eventually failed. In the early 1900's, archeologists discovered the first remnants of these forts. Along with the rich history, you can enjoy a walk on the nature path, where you may see a WWII relic as you make your way through the marsh. View the landmark at the end of the boardwalk and look for additional information about these settlements in the museum.

Douglas Visitors' Center

You should first visit the Douglas Visitors' Center, named after Paul H. Douglas who graduated from Marine Corps Boot camp at the age of 50. A plaque outside the center gives a brief synopsis of Paul Douglas's amazing achievements. Once inside, find the form for your new Marine's platoon. Check-in by signing your name, the number of visitors and a phone number where you can be reached. You should check-in only once. The Visitors' Center has a small gift shop and an area to sign up for specialty items like engraved commemorative bricks and graduation DVDs.

Drill Instructor Monument

A monument to all drill instructors was dedicated April 24, 1999, and resides near the Peatross Parade Deck on Blvd de France. Many of the bricks are engraved with the names and dates of service of past drill instructors; step in the footprints and read the Drill Instructors' Creed.

Drill Instructor School

The DI School is on the corner of Panama and Santo Domingo Streets. Often, as I drive by the school, there are groups of Marines practicing close order drill and reviewing their techniques of military training tasks.

Dry Dock

Sometimes after lunch, my husband and I would take a stroll around the area. During our walks, we would explore the late 19th century dry dock.

I would imagine a large ship pulling into the dock for repair with workers filling a floating caisson gate with water so it would sink and close off the Beaufort River, then draining the water out of the dock, and patching-up the vessel. With this repair, water could flow back in to the dock. I would then imagine the caisson gate filling up with air and being towed away to allow the ship to move on to other destinations.

Seeing a large rectangular area filled with water on a humid summer day gave folks another idea. There are historical pictures showing people enjoying a swim in the dry dock using it as a saltwater swimming pool. Now fenced and concealed behind brush, it remains a historic landmark where fiddler crabs scurry around the mud and vegetation.

Elliott's Beach

Elliott's Beach is a beach with a pavilion, covered picnic tables, children's playground, bench swings and three port-o-potties. You cannot swim there, but the views of the ocean are pretty. If you decide to picnic in the area keep in mind that Marine Corps Community Service (MCCS) reserves the pavilion, covered picnic tables, bench swings and children's playground for qualified patrons. If a group booked the beach for an event, you might have to make other arrangements. Fortunately, there are many other picnic sites available.

The Gazebo

Built it in the early 1900's, the gazebo endured the elements, including a few hurricanes. Because of weathering and damage over time, band performances on the gazebo ceased. With renovations completed in 2017 I am hopeful the MCRD PI Marine band will be back up on the stage soon, playing Sousa marches for the crowd.

With its Victorian style architecture, it is easy to envision the PI Marine Band playing a concert on the gazebo while people sit in folding chairs and eat snacks on picnic blankets as they listen to the music. Mike played a few concerts there long ago.

Iron Mike

Guarding the corner of Blvd de France and Santo Domingo, and poised for action stands Iron Mike, a bronze monument erected for all of the Parris Island Marines who sacrificed their lives in service to our country during World War I.

Iwo Jima Monument.

The Parris Island's Iwo Jima Monument, constructed prior to the end of WWII, accompanied dignitaries around the country to promote the War Bond campaign. After the war, the sculptor, Mr. Felix de Weldon, donated it to Parris Island, but the Monument was never intended to be a permanent outdoor exhibit. Before 2016, you could see exposed plaster and concrete from under the bronze coloring. During July 2015, renovations began and continued until the unveiling on March 14, 2016. Make sure to get a picture with your new Marine in front of this iconic statue! Please do not allow children to climb on the structure.

Leatherneck Square

Ask your new Marine to show you the confidence course and where some of his MCMAP training took place in Leatherneck Square. Imagine a platoon of recruits attacking the obstacles.

Legends Golf Course

If you have time, bring your golf clubs and enjoy a round of golf right on Parris Island. Otherwise, drive by and stop at the Sand Trap grill for a bite to eat. If you enjoy early American history, make sure you visit the archeological sites of Charles Fort, Santa Elena, and Fort San Marcos.

Lyceum

Originally, Family Day buffets and Command dinners were held here. However, in 2016, Hurricane Matthew damaged the building. Now it is closed until repairs are made. So the lunches and Command dinners have been temporarily moved to Traditions Restaurant a historical building with fabulous views of the marsh.

I have many fond memories of the Lyceum. This building has been used for many events, including many USMC Birthday Balls and Christmas concerts performed by the Parris Island Marine Band. Once we attended a 1940's style performance by the Ladies for Liberty, a singing trio reminiscent of the Andrew Sisters. Even though updates to the building have taken place over the years, it continues to generate a vibe that harkens back to the early 20th century.

Molly Marine

In the center of a small park area on Blvd de France, you will notice a bronze statue dedicated October 23, 1999, honoring all female Marines. The Parris Island Molly Marine is a replica of a statue erected in 1943 in New Orleans created specifically to aid in female recruitment efforts.

The Marine Corps Exchange (MCX)

The MCX opens at 0600 (6:00 a.m.) Monday through Friday. You should have time to stop by between events. At this time, family members can eat at the food court and purchase items from the souvenir section and sundries section. Anything else must be obtained by an authorized patron.

Page Field

The field finished in 1934 and named after Capt. Arthur H. Page, Jr., a Marine pilot who received the Distinguished Flying Cross, originally was an airfield during WWII. It is now used for recruit training.

Parris Island Bowling Center

The bowling center is in the same building as Subway, building 203. If you are staying on base, consider bowling as an after-dinner activity. Call ahead for the hours of operation 843-228-1551.

Parris Island Museum & Gift Shop

Dedicated January 8, 1975, as the Marine Corps first Command Museum, the museum is located on Panama Street. Inside you will find information and displays depicting the rich history of Parris Island from long ago before it belonged to the Marine Corps to present day Marine Corp history. I visited the museum on many occasions since 1994, and I enjoy going back again and again. There is always more to see and explore so give yourself plenty of time when you go.

Peatross Parade Deck

The outdoor graduation ceremony takes place on this deck, named after Major General Oscar F. Peatross who served in WWII, Korea, and Vietnam. You will find a plaque with more information about him by the Parade Deck. The area is also called The Grinder due to the sand and mud one had to march through back in the days before the deck was paved.

Purple Heart Monument

The monument, dedicated in 2008 to honor all Purple Heart recipients, is located by the Peatross Parade deck.

Picnic Areas on Base

As you drive onto the base, after exiting the second turnoff of the traffic circle, you will see a Wildlife Watchable area where you can eat with a view of Third Battalion Pond. If the covered picnic area is occupied, go across the street to find more picnic benches, grills and a restroom. Travel a bit farther down the road onto the next causeway for one more picnic area on the left. You will have to drive to these two picnic spots, but they provide a more secluded natural setting than the grounds closer to the Parade Deck. Don't forget insect repellent.

Alongside the MCX, there are plenty of picnic tables to enjoy the food you brought or food purchased from the exchange. There are also tables inside at the food court and a few covered seating areas just outside the exchange.

There are picnic tables outside the Douglas Visitors' Center and in the grassy area across the street. Keep in mind this is a high traffic area and many people will be walking about as you eat.

The Bunker, in building 113 on Olongapo Street, is currently open from 1000 to 1500 (10:00 a.m. to 3:00 p.m.) on Family Day. Escape from the heat (or cold depending on the time of year) and eat your lunch inside where they have places to sit and vending machines.

Quarters One

This is the home for Parris Island's Commanding General. It was built in the late 1800's and renovated many times, most recently for the 100th Anniversary of Parris Island which the Marine Corps Recruit Depot, celebrated in October 2015. I visited the home once for a Christmas party. Although it has over 6000 square feet of living area, it retains a cozy feeling to each room. I remember admiring the large kitchen and the wrap-around porch. You will not be permitted to tour the inside, but you can drive by and appreciate the architecture.

Recruit Chapel

Every week, recruits may attend religious services at the Recruit Chapel. The Warrior's Prayer on Family day is scheduled there. While you visit, take some time to admire the beautiful stained glass windows depicting Marines and various religious themes.

Restroom Locations

There are plenty of bathrooms around the base. When you stop at the Douglas Visitors' Center, you will find restrooms on the first and second floors.

At the Peatross Parade Deck where outdoor graduations and other events are held, there are restrooms behind the stadium seating. In the female head (a military term for bathroom), I found ten regular stalls and one handicapped stall.

The Marine Corps Exchange has restrooms by the food court. You will also find restroom facilities at Traditions Restaurant, Brig and Brew, Sand Trap Grill, The Lyceum, Subway/Bowling Alley, The Parris Island Museum and The Bunker.

In addition there are port-o-potties at Elliott's Beach and the Horse Island picnic site. The restroom is in a wooded area away from main activities so bring some toilet paper just in case they are out.

Rifle Range

When you hear pop, pop, pop sounds in the early morning, you are listening to recruits and/or permanent personnel firing on one of the ranges at Weapon's Battalion. The ranges have been in continuous use since WWI era, which I witnessed when I briefly assisted a professor in collecting core samples of the wetlands. The samples contained spent rounds from various weapons captured in the mud from WWI to present day!

Souvenir Penny Coin Machine Locations

Have two quarters and a shiny penny on hand to put through the souvenir coin machine and watch your penny become a Parris Island souvenir. My daughter used to collect these and keep them in a special holder. If you like them too, you will find one at the Douglas Visitors' Center, one at the Marine Corps Exchange and one at the Parris Island Museum. Get one for your collection and one for a friend back home.

Adapt and Overcome Action Steps:
- ☐ Visit the ParrisIsland.com Pinterest boards to see pictures of MCRD Parris Island.

Summary of Main Points:
- Parris Island has several things to see and do from historical landmarks, to eating places, to important military buildings.

CHAPTER 13

Graduation Day Events

In the last analysis, what the Marine Corps becomes is what we make of it during our respective watches. And that watch of each Marine is not confined to the time he spends on active duty. It lasts as long as he is "proud to bear the title of United States Marine."

General Louis H. Wilson, Jr.
26th Commandant of the Marine Corps

Chapter Questions:
- How much time should I allow to get onto the base?
- Is it worth my time to see morning colors?
- Will I have time to view morning colors?
- Will there be a security check for the graduation?

On Graduation day, there will be pictures to take, banners to wave and don't forget hugs and kisses afterward. Everything you have done up to this point prepared you and your family members to enjoy the graduation. In this chapter I will discuss when to arrive, attending the Colors Ceremony and making your way to the graduation ceremony. By the end of this chapter, you should feel confident about what to expect and what you will be doing on Grad Day.

When to Arrive

Expect to arrive 45 minutes early to allow plenty of time for parking. Bring a camera, appropriate outerwear for the weather conditions, a hat and a seat cushion to keep you comfortable on the bleachers. Make sure to apply sunscreen to your face, arms and legs, especially in the spring and summer. It is always good to have bug spray along too just in case. One never knows how bad the sand fleas will be until they show up.

During winter ensure you have warm clothing to walk around to include a hat and gloves. Remember the temperature may be a little colder, and it is windier on the island than it is in Beaufort. Wear comfortable shoes for walking. Check the weather before you leave. It may be warmer than you expect (we've had weather in the upper 70's during December), or colder because of a front moving into the area.

Morning Colors

Each day on every Marine Corps Post throughout the world, Marines hoist morning colors. Morning colors, the traditional flag raising ceremony, occurs each day at 0800 (8:00 a.m.) as per U.S. Navy regulations. Evening colors occur when the flag is lowered at sunset. When the flag is carried by foot, they call it the National Colors. It has other names depending on how it is being displayed.

Some people worry about having enough time to get to the graduation ceremony if they go to the Colors Ceremony. You should have sufficient time to do both, and the Colors Ceremony is something worth your effort.

Everyone assembles in front of Barrow Hall by 0745 (7:45 a.m.). The color detail carries the flag to the flagpole and attaches the grommets to the halyard (rope) snaps. During this time the Parris Island Marine Corps Band plays. Please applaud if you enjoy their music; they appreciate your support. At 0755 (7:55 a.m.), they sound the first call. At this point there is time for one more musical selection. A moment before 0800 (8:00 a.m.), you will hear the band sound attention, a Marine strikes the bell eight times, and the band plays the National Anthem as the flag is hoisted. Upon completion of the National Anthem Carry On is sounded. The band plays additional martial music as the color detail secures the halyard. The officer on deck (in attendance) will speak to those in attendance, many times it is the Commanding General.

The Colors Ceremony takes place from 0745 to 0815 (7:45 a.m. to 8:15 a.m.) unless it rains hard enough to cancel the ceremony. Arrive early enough to allow for parking and travel to the headquarters area seating. Once you park, make your way over to the tram. If you have time, stop and get a cup of coffee at the Java Café before taking the tram or walking to the Commanding General's Building. Find a seat on the bleachers. Take out your seat cushion, if you have one, and relax until the ceremony begins.

Graduation Ceremony

After Morning Colors, make your way to the Peatross Parade Deck for the Graduation Ceremony. If the weather is bad, you will be instructed to meet at another location. Expect a little wait as you go through security. Make sure any medication you have on your person is in the original prescription bottle with the proper label. Do not bring anything which may be considered a weapon and don't bring things you don't need. Once through security, you will be directed towards seating.

The Parris Island Marine Band will march onto the Parade Deck marking the start of the Graduation Ceremony. Look at your program for the sequence of events. If you would like to see a

sample program, visit
http://www.mcrdpi.marines.mil/gradprogram/

The ceremony lasts one hour ending with the final dismissal.

Adapt and Overcome Action Steps:
- ☐ Make a list of the things you need to bring along on Graduation Day.
- ☐ Pack everything up the night before so you are ready to leave early in the morning.
- ☐ Figure out how long it takes to get to the Parris Island exit then add 45 minutes onto your travel time.
- ☐ Don't miss the emotionally moving Colors Ceremony.
- ☐ Make your way to the Parade Deck as soon as Colors is over.
- ☐ Enjoy the Graduation!
- ☐ Download extra copies of the graduation program.

Summary of Main Points:
- Arrive 45 minutes early to ensure you have time for parking.
- Take the time to attend the Colors Ceremony.
- Make sure to only bring necessary items.

What's Next?

Typically new Marines have 10 days of leave after completing Boot camp. After leave most will report to the School of Infantry (SOI). The last page of the Graduation Ceremony handout contains information about what they need when reporting to SOI East, including what uniform to wear, what uniforms to pack and how to dress when traveling to the school. See the current SOI web page for more information.
https://www.trngcmd.marines.mil/Units/South-Atlantic/SOI-E/

I hope you found this planner useful as you began your journey into the Marine Corps family. You worked hard to keep in touch with your recruit as he trained to become United States Marine and now your role becomes even more important. There will be new challenges, new rewards and new obstacles to overcome, but with the strong support of loved ones, your Marine will excel and enjoy a rewarding career. I wish you safe travels as you return home.

Congratulations and welcome to our family!

Semper Fidelis

What did you think of the Parris Island Planner?

Thank you for purchasing the Parris Island Planner. I hope it helped you better understand what goes on during boot camp and how you can be your recruit's best support person. If you enjoyed this book I would love to hear from you and I hope you will take time to post a review on Amazon. Your feedback will help me keep the planner current and complete.

Thank you for your support.

Please leave a review of this book at www.amazon.com

Don't Forget Your Free Bonus Gift!

As a thank you for purchasing the Parris Island Planner I am giving you a bonus gift:

The workbook includes checklists and worksheets to go along with the Adapt and Overcome Action Steps in the planner. To get your workbook go to the web address below.

https://www.parrisisland.com/workbook/

Appendix A

Military Glossary

Administrative Black Flag – This condition exists when the Branch Medical Clinic and the battalion aid stations cannot handle any more heat injuries. During an administrative black flag, all training stops.

AHSS – Automated Heat Stress System

AOR – Area of Responsibility

ASVAB - Armed Services Vocational Aptitude Battery

AWOL – Absence Without Leave

AWTF – All Weather Training Facility, a building located on Parris Island

BAQ – Basic Allowance for Quarters

BHA – Basic Housing Allowance

BEQ – Bachelor Enlisted Quarters

B&U – Boots and Utilities (also known as boots and uts)

Billeted – Where Marines are housed

BMC – Branch Medical Clinic

Brig – Jail

BWT – Basic Warrior Training

BZO – Battle Sight Zero

Cam/Cvr/Concel – Camouflage/Cover/Conceal

Cammies – Camouflage uniform

CFT – Combat Fitness Test

Cbt Cond – Combat Conditioning

Cold SOP – Cold Weather Standard Operating Procedures

Commissary – A grocery store located on a military base

CO – Commanding Officer

Cover – What a Marine calls his hat. There are several different kinds of covers e.g. blue's cover, barracks cover, garrison cover, etc…

Chevrons – Inverted v-shaped insignia indicating rank of enlisted personnel

Crucible – the culmination of all recruit training in which recruits must endure a 54-hour field training exercise that tests everything they have learned over the past three months, overcoming obstacles and working together as a team in order to complete various missions

CRT/CRS – Circuit Course

CVD – Core Value Discussions – Classes given during boot camp

DEP – Delayed Entry Program

Devil Dogs – nickname given to Marines during WWI by German soldiers. "Teufel Hunde"

DECA – Defense Commissary Agency

Deck – A naval term that refers to the surface of a ship. In the Marine Corps it means the floor.

DEERS – Defense Enrollment Eligibility Reporting System

DFAS – Defense Finance and Accounting System

DI – Drill Instructor

DITY Move – Do It Yourself Move

DOD – Department of Defense

DON – Department of the Navy

Dry Firing – Firing weapons without ammunition

EGL – Eagle, Globe and Anchor – The Marine Corps emblem.

EOS – End of Obligated Service

EAS – End of Active Service

Esprit de corps – Definition from www.merriam-webster.com, Merriam-Webster's dictionary, as the common spirit existing in the members of a group and inspiring enthusiasm, devotion and strong regard for the honor of the group.

Fast rope – to slide down a rope suspended from a swing arm on the MCRD PI rappel tower as if one were coming out of a helicopter.

FOB – Forward Operating Base

Good Scoop – Reliable information

Grass Week – The week before the rifle range which is spent sitting in the grass, getting classes and dry firing

Guidon – The flag being held by the guide in a formation. Guidon colors are yellow and red for every platoon.

Hat – Nickname for a drill instructor. Recruits should never refer to a DI as a Hat.

Hatch – Door

Head – Naval term for bathroom

Heavy – Experienced drill instructor, second to the Senior DI

Hot SOP – Hot weather Standard Operating Procedures

IFAK – Initial First Aid Kit

INNOCS – Inoculations

Iron Ducks – Recruits who can't swim

IST – Initial Strength Test – a physical test consisting of a 1.5-mile run, crunches, pull-ups for men and the flex arm hang for women.

IED – Improvised Explosive Device

Jar Head – A derogatory slang word for Marines. The origin may be because of their haircuts.

JROTC – Junior Reserve Officers' Training Corps

KA-BAR – A combat knife made popular during WWII when it became one of the standard issue fighting knives of the Marine Corps.

Kill Hat – Drill instructor who delivers incentive training

L/F – Lead Series/Follow Series – During boot camp, companies are split up into two groups. One called Lead Series the other called Follow Series.

Leatherneck – A term used to describe Marines because of the leather collars worn from 1775-1875

MARADMIN – Marine Corps Administrative Message

MCMAP – Marine Corps Martial Arts Program

MCT – Marine Combat Training

MCX – Marine Corps Exchange – a Marine base store

MEPS – Military Entrance Processing Station

Mess Hall – The same as a chow hall, a dining area for Marines

MOS – Military Occupational Specialty

MRE – Meal Ready to Eat

MTU – Marksmanship Training Unit

MWR – Moral, Welfare and Recreation

NCO – Non-Commissioned Officer

NJP – Non-Judicial Punishment

OIC – Officer in Charge

OOD – Officer of the Day

ORM – Operational Risk Management

PCU – Physical Conditioning Unit

PCS – Permanent Change of Station

PFC – Private First Class

PFT – Physical Fitness Test

Plt – Platoon

PME – Professional Military Education

Poolee – Someone who is in the Delayed Entry Program (DEP) waiting to go into boot camp.

POV – Privately Owned Vehicle

P1-P3 – Found on the training matrix, P stands for processing days – Processing involves getting uniforms, gear, haircuts and a medical evaluation

PT – Physical Training

PTAD – Permissive Temporary Assignment of Duty

PFT – Physical Fitness Test

PX– Post Exchange – A store located on a Marine base

Pugil Sticks – Training sticks with padding on the ends. They represent rifles with fixed bayonets and are used to simulate a close encounter with the enemy

Rack – A bed

Recruit Crud – Cold-like infections resulting from poolies who come from different areas living in close quarters during training.

Recycle – A term used for recruits who fail to master a graduation requirement and must undergo additional instruction.

RTB – Recruit Training Battalion

RTR - Recruit Training Regiment

Sand Fleas – Tiny gnat like insects that bite.

Scoop – Slang for information

SDI – Senior Drill Instructor

Semper Fidelis – Latin for always faithful – the Marine Corps motto. Often abbreviated as Semper Fi.

SOI - School of Infantry

Squad Bay – Living quarters

Squared Away – Everything in order

SRB – Service Record Book

SNCOIC – Staff Non-Commissioned Officer-in-Charge

TAD – Temporary Assignment of Duty

Team Week – A time during boot camp when recruits help around the base

TIG - Time in Grade

UA – Unauthorized Absence

UCMJ – Uniform Code of Military Justice

WFTBn – Weapons and Field Training Battalion

Appendix B

Letter Writing Templates

Print out the following templates and use them to spark ideas for the next letter to your recruit. Pick and choose a couple of the paragraphs for each letter. Pop in a few extra first class postage stamps with your letter and a self-addressed envelope if you like.

TEMPLATE 1 – FROM A PARENT

Today's Date

Dear [Insert Recruit's First Name],

How are things in paradise? What do you think of your buddies in the platoon?

Since you left [insert relative] has [insert activity]. We all think it is [insert reaction].

Last week we went over to [insert relatives], they haven't changed much. Maybe we can visit them after you graduate.

The other day we saw [insert friends name]. He asked how you were doing. What should we tell him?

The [insert team name] [insert won/lost] last week. [Add a sentence or two about his favorite players]. I hope you like the news article I am sending about the team.

We went to [insert concert or performance]. The [group/band] sounded great.

Your [sister/brother] has been [insert a sentence or two about what they've been up to lately].

There is a new [insert video game] coming out next month. We know how much you loved playing [insert name of favorite video game and add a few sentences about the game]

How are you doing? Do you need us to send anything?

We have a copy of the Training Matrix. It shows you may be [insert event] this week. How did it go?
For example: Rifle range qualifications are coming up. Are you looking forward to firing? [If your family hunts you can add a paragraph or two about a previous trip].

I've heard the chow hall food is good. What do you think of it? Are you getting enough to eat?

A new season of your [insert favorite show] starts next week. On Saturday they ran a marathon of last season. We recorded them for you to watch again and we set up the machine to record all of the new episodes. Now you won't miss any of them while you are away. [Add a sentence or two about his favorite characters but be careful not to reveal any new plot twists]

That's all the news for this week. I [we] will write again soon. We are so proud of you! Keep your spirits up, there are only [insert number of weeks left] until you graduate.

Love and miss you,
[Sign name(s)]

TEMPLATE 2 – FROM A GRANDPARENT

Dear [Enter grandson's first name],

Remember when your grandfather and I used to take you to the [insert place (beach, park, mall etc....) and time (summer, fall etc...)? Add a few descriptive sentences about the trip (for example: The days we spent building sand castles and swimming in the ocean seem like yesterday.) Now it is [add a sentence or two about the way it changed or did not change since you last went].

Last week we saw [insert movie name] at the movie theater. [Add a sentence or two about the parts you liked or didn't like. Just don't give away any plot secrets.] You should [see/not see] it. The last time we took you to a movie you [insert a few sentences about your experience]. You always loved eating [insert favorite movie candy or popcorn]. Maybe you could see a show with us after boot camp.

[Insert family member name(s)] visited last week. [Insert a sentence about the visit]

Did you know that your [insert mom or dad] [insert funny story from the past] when he was little?

We still go to [insert high school] to see the [insert sports activity like track, football or soccer] games. Your friend [insert friends name and how he is doing on the team]. Would you like us to give him your address the next time we see him?

Grandad still eats at [insert restaurant name]. I think he expects you to come out of the kitchen and say hello. I bet you don't miss that job one bit.

I've heard the food is pretty good at the chow hall, but you must miss home cooked meals. Stop by after you graduate and I will make you your favorite [insert cake, lasagna, etc...]

Everyone is so proud of you and we hope you are doing well. Please write soon and let us know if you need anything.

Love,

[sign name(s)]

Additional Letter Writing Prompts:

Talk about a family pet. Who is watching it? Talk about something amusing the pet did. Keep it positive.

Mention something about his favorite comic books, or a new book that is out now.

Does your recruit like crossword puzzles, word searches? Find one or two and send them in your next letter.

If your recruit has brothers and sisters, nieces and nephews or other close relatives, write a paragraph or two about recent activities like class plays, sporting events, or something cute his niece did last week.

Is there something new going on in the neighborhood?

Remember when you were little you used to ….

Appendix C

Hyperlinks used in the Parris Island Planner

Basic Warrior Training (BWT) Article
https://www.parrisisland.com/1065/pi023-recruits-learn-combat-basics-on-parris-island/

Brig and Brew
http://www.mccs-sc.com/rec-fit/brignbrew.shtml

Crucible Video
https://www.youtube.com/watch?v=ikSHI7RxyCM

Eating on base
https://www.parrisisland.com/eating-on-base/

MCCS
http://www.mccs-sc.com/mil-fam/recruit/index.shtml

EventBrite
https://www.eventbrite.com/o/mcrd-parris-island-graduation-week-activities-amp-events-1920813227

Family Day Schedule
https://www.parrisisland.com/family-day-events/

Firearms on base
http://www.mcrdpi.marines.mil/Visitors/FAQ/#q8

Graduation Programs
https://www.mcrdpi.marines.mil/Resources/Graduation-Info/Graduation-Program/

IST Requirements
https://www.marines.com/become-a-marine/requirements/physical-fitness.html

Marines YouTube Channel
https://www.youtube.com/user/marines/search?query=recruit+training+parris+island

MCCS Graduation Activities and Events page
http://www.mccs-sc.com/mil-fam/recruit/index.shtml

Morning Colors music
http://www.marineband.marines.mil/Audio-Resources/Ceremonial-Music/#section2

National Weather Service - Beaufort area forecast
http://forecast.weather.gov/MapClick.php?lat=32.3495&lon=-80.6775#.WiAxzFWnHIU

The National Weather Service
www.weather.gov

Official MCRD PI Facebook Page
https://www.facebook.com/ParrisIsland/

ParrisIsland.com Pinterest Boards
https://www.pinterest.com/MCRDPI/boards/

ParrisIsland.com Places to Stay
https://www.parrisisland.com/places-to-stay/

Policy for dogs
http://www.mcrdpi.marines.mil/Visitors/FAQ/#q27

Rank Structure
http://www.marines.mil/Marines/Ranks.aspx

Receiving Video
https://www.youtube.com/watch?v=vXwxvzvCWj4

Requirements to get on base
http://www.mcrdpi.marines.mil/Visitors/Coming-To-Parris-Island/

RV Park
http://www.mccs-sc.com/din-lod/rvpark.shtml

Sign up page for free workbook
https://www.parrisisland.com/workbook/

SOI
https://www.trngcmd.marines.mil/Units/South-Atlantic/SOI-E/

Training Matrix
https://www.mcrdpi.marines.mil/Recruit-Training/Recruit-Training-Matrix/

Bibliography

100 Years of Making Marines at Marine Corps Recruit Depot Parris Island, South Carolina. First Edition 2014 PCN – 106000100000

2017 Educator's Workshop Command Brief

A Few Good Quotes from The Marine Corps Commandant, http://www.washingtonexaminer.com/a-few-good-quotes-from-the-marine-corps-commandant (accessed November 19, 2017).

A History of the Women Marines 1946-1977, by Col Mary V. Stremlow, U. S. Marine Corps Reserve, History and Museums Division, Headquarters, U. S. Marine Corps, Washington DC, 1986. p. 124

Champie, Elmore A. (1958). A Brief History of the Marine Corps Base and Recruit Depot, Parris Island, South Carolina, 1891–1956 (PDF). Washington, D.C.: Historical Branch, United States Marine Corps)

Depot Order P1510.31 Standing Operating Procedures for Recruit Training

Marine Corps Historical Reference Series, #1, A Brief History of the United States Marine Corps, Major Norman W. Hicks, USMC, Historical Branch, G-3 Division, Headquarters, US Marine Corps, Washington D.C. 1961

Marine Corps Order (MCO) 1510.32 Recruit Training dated 20 Dec 2012

Marine Corps Order, (MCO) P1510.31 Standing Operating Procedures for Recruit Training, 20 Mar 2014

Marine Corps Order (MCO) 3574.2K Marine Corps Combat Marksmanship Programs 01 Aug 2007

Marine Corps Order (MCO) 5060.20, Marine Corps Drill and Ceremonies Manual, dated 5 May 2003

National Register of Historic Places Inventory – Nomination Form – Dry Dock and Commanding General's House, June 30, 1978.

Office of Communication Strategy and Operations, MCRD, Parris Island, SC

Operational Risk Management 130736 Student Handout

The Marine Corps Training Matrix

Unites States Marines Graduation Ceremony Pamphlet 31 March 2017

ABOUT THE AUTHOR

Photo by Michael Basilone

Vera Basilone lives in Beaufort South Carolina with her husband
Michael and Mr. Winston the dachshund.

Mess with one Marine and you
Mess with them all.

Dios está contigo.
You are braver than you believe
Stronger than you seem.
and Smarter Than you Think

My son risks His life to save
strangers, Just imagine What
He would do to protect me.

Made in the USA
Middletown, DE
15 February 2023

24967310R00080